PATENTLY SUCCESSFUL

PATENTLY SUCCESSFUL

Understanding and Mastering Intellectual Property

NICOLE REINEKE

Columbia Business School Publishing

Columbia University Press
Publishers Since 1893
New York   Chichester, West Sussex
cup.columbia.edu

Library of Congress Cataloging-in-Publication Data
Names: Reineke, Nicole author
Title: Patently successful : understanding and mastering intellectual property / Nicole Reineke.
Description: New York, NY : Columbia University Press, 2026. | Includes index.
Identifiers: LCCN 2026009521 | ISBN 9780231223829 hardback | ISBN 9780231565219 ebook | ISBN 9780231567701 PDF
Subjects: LCSH: Intellectual property—United States | Patent laws and legislation—United States | Artificial intelligence—Law and legislation—United States | Technological innovations—Law and legislation—United States
Classification: LCC KF2979 .R45 2026
LC record available at https://lccn.loc.gov/2026009521

Cover image by Julia Zichello and Rachel Harvie

Illustrations by Rachel Harvie

GPSR Authorized Representative: Easy Access System Europe, Mustamäe tee 50, 10621 Tallinn, Estonia, gpsr.requests@easproject.com

CONTENTS

INTRODUCTION

The Power of Intellectual Property (IP)

The job market can feel like an overcrowded place. You feel surrounded by people vying for the same opportunities, promotions, and recognition. I often witness the frustration and stress of new graduates struggling to find internships and first jobs, as well as experienced professionals searching for mid- and late-stage employment after a layoff.

How can you thrive under these circumstances? I was fortunate to realize early in my career that creating and owning intellectual property (IP) helps us rise above the noise and differentiate ourselves. IP is power. It's one way to take control of your story, create a distinct identity that sets you apart, and navigate an uncertain world by creating a space where your ideas are protected and valued. Whether you're just starting out and looking to stand out, or you're a seasoned professional ready to cement your legacy, this book is for you. It's a guide for those who want to use IP to grow their careers, gain influence, and unlock new opportunities.

Here is a secret: You do not have to be an inventor to create IP.

IP is more than patents; it's your evidence of expertise, a tangible record of your contributions, and a key that opens doors to recognition, promotions, and new roles. Most importantly, IP is something that you create and control. You don't have to wait for anyone to hand you an opportunity. It's your way to move beyond the stereotypes and judgments that might hold you back, and it becomes a badge of expertise that speaks for itself.

INTELLECTUAL PROPERTY (IP)

IP, or intellectual property, is proof that you know what you're talking about. It's how you turn your ideas into something real—something that can be seen, shared, and valued. IP is not just for those in the high-tech industry. Anyone can create and leverage it.

Yes, IP includes patents, copyrights, trademarks, and trade secrets. But in the context of your career, it's also the articles you write, the talks you give, the open-source code you contribute to, and the standards you help shape. It's evidence of your expertise and you control it. IP is your voice, made visible.

An IP portfolio is a collection of IP and activities that show the world what you've built. It's how you start creating recognition. It's a way to stand out, grow your career, mentor others, and leave a legacy of impact.

By thinking of IP as a journey, we begin to see that it's much more than just legal protection. It's about building your foundation, creating a community, mentoring the next generation, and leaving a legacy that extends beyond yourself. Each patent, publication, or contribution becomes tangible proof of the difference you've made.

Consider your current situation. You may have a job, be enrolled in a class, or engage in meaningful conversations with friends or family. These are all sources of ideas. And ideas are the

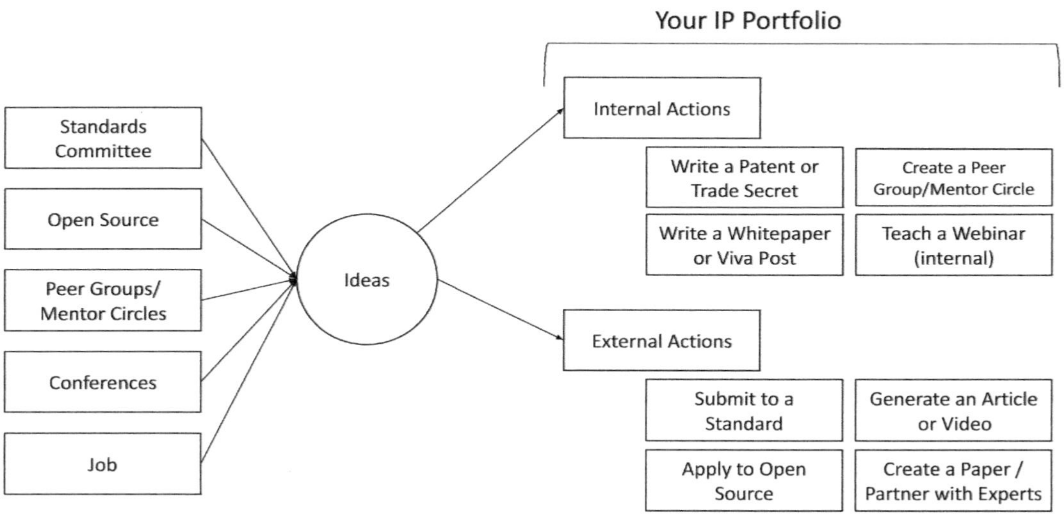

FIGURE 0.1 Turning ideas into IP. (Illustration by Nicole Reineke.)

starting point for generating intellectual property—both within your current role and beyond it.

As shown in the diagram, when you engage actively (participating in a standards committee, contributing to open source, joining peer groups, attending conferences, or even just doing your job) you expose yourself to new perspectives, problems, and possibilities. These spark ideas. And from those ideas, you can take meaningful action that will build your personal IP portfolio.

There are two primary paths forward when you learn something new or have an idea: internal actions and external actions. Internal actions might include writing a patent or trade secret, creating a mentor circle, publishing within your current organization, or teaching a webinar. These are things that impact your current role or peer groups. External actions could involve submitting to a standard, generating public-facing content like an article or video, applying to open-source projects, or collaborating with experts on a paper.

All of these steps help you build your IP portfolio and your reputation. With each action, you generate *evidence of your expertise*, helping you grow your career, expand your influence, and contribute to the larger professional community. The more ideas you have and follow up on, the more opportunities you will have.

Throughout this book, you'll learn how to generate powerful ideas and establish your expertise through IP. Each chapter is designed to build upon the last, guiding you step by step—from discovering your unique value to influencing your industry:

1. **IP Journeys**—We begin with the stories of extraordinary individuals, some of the most prolific and influential inventors, IP creators, mentors, and community builders of our time. Their paths reveal how curiosity, persistence, and collaboration shape lasting impact.

2. **Sparking Ideas That Become IP**—Innovation starts with identifying what truly needs fixing. This chapter shows you how to uncover meaningful problems, reframe challenges as opportunities, and apply structured creativity to develop solutions that form the foundation of IP.
3. **IP in Depth**—Here, we'll explore each major type of IP—patents, trade secrets, copyrights, trademarks, open source, and standards—in depth. You'll learn how to generate each one, how they work together, and how to decide which type best protects your ideas and advances your goals.
4. **Intentional Pursuit of IP**—In this chapter, we design your customized IP road map. You'll learn how to build your support system, create mentor circles (one of my biggest secrets to success), and set goals that translate your ideas into tangible outcomes.
5. **The Role of Generative AI in Creating IP**—Artificial intelligence has changed how we create, analyze, and protect ideas. We'll explore the opportunities and risks of using AI to generate IP and how to ensure your innovations remain authentically, and legally, yours.
6. **Leveraging IP for Professional Growth**—Your IP portfolio can be one of the most powerful tools for career advancement. This chapter outlines practical ways to use IP to position yourself for promotions, new roles, and increased visibility across your field.
7. **Using IP to Challenge and Influence Industry Norms**—Here, we'll examine how IP can be used to challenge outdated norms, shape industry standards, and drive systemic change. You'll see how thought leadership and advocacy can turn your ideas into movements.
8. **Challenges You May Encounter**—No journey is without obstacles. From time constraints and self-doubt to organizational

bias and legal complexity, we'll discuss common challenges and how to navigate them with confidence and persistence.

Appendixes: Tools to Get You Started—The appendixes include a practical workbook designed to help you put everything you've learned into action. It's your step-by-step guide to planning, documenting, and executing your IP journey.

This isn't just a technical guide; it's a call to action. Throughout these pages, you'll find strategies, real-life examples, and practical steps. This information will help you create and protect IP, leverage it for career advancement, and use it to mentor others and drive change. You'll learn how to build a plan to pursue IP, how to navigate obstacles, and how to make sure your work gets noticed.

To guide us on this journey, I'm about to introduce you to individuals whose wisdom, resilience, and vision are a master class in achieving long-term goals and making a profound impact on the lives of others. They were gracious enough to sit with me and share their stories. Each of them has a unique background, approach, and set of lessons to share.

I have always been wary of the word *mentor*. For a long time, I wasn't sure what it truly meant, or whether I had ever had one. But with reflection, I've come to understand its intent. In the context of this book, a mentor is someone who has meaningfully influenced my personal path: someone whose insight, example, or belief in me shifted the direction of my own thinking. My mentors happen to be from the high-tech space, but this process and these stories are applicable to any industry.

A commonality among these mentors was that, at a pivotal moment in their journeys, most of them came to a major realization: they had goals that were larger than their job, and without focused attention these goals would remain unattainable. This clarity became a compass, helping them navigate the complexities of their work. Yet clarity alone was not enough. Barriers inevitably arose, sometimes in the form of external resistance, other times in the form of internal doubts, and all too frequently in the form of systemic challenges. Their drive and determination allowed them to confront these obstacles head-on and continue making progress, often against the odds.

One thing that continually surprises me is how people see themselves. So many people are unaware of the extent of their impact, even those who have objectively reached incredible heights in their careers. It's easy to view someone else's achievements as monumental while dismissing one's own as ordinary. This discrepancy is critical to acknowledge, not just because it reminds us of the humanity behind every success, but because it encourages us to reflect on our own impact. Perhaps the things we take for granted in ourselves are the very qualities that inspire others.

One of my favorite quotes from my conversations with these IP mentors came from Bill Pfeifer, the person who connected me to one of the highlights of my career: a project with National Geographic. He said, almost casually, "I don't think I'm great at this. I just do what I do. I don't know. Sometimes it's good." His words struck me deeply because they reflect a mindset that many of us share: we underestimate our accomplishments while simultaneously achieving extraordinary things.

What we should take from this is essential: we are all human, we are all complex, and we are all on our own journeys. Sometimes, we do good things. And when we figure out what those things are, it's a gift to ourselves and the world to find ways to do them more often. These moments of clarity and impact don't just propel our careers forward; they create opportunities that uplift others. If we can learn to identify, nurture, and celebrate these contributions, we improve ourselves and empower those around us.

This theme runs through the stories of the mentors in this book. Despite their humility, they have made incredible contributions through technical innovation and their capacity to connect, mentor, and inspire. Their impact, whether they see it clearly or not, is undeniable. As we explore their journeys, we may uncover ways to better see and amplify our own.

On a personal note, each of these mentors has profoundly influenced my career and life. Their guidance has been invaluable, shaping the way I think, work, and even the existence of this book—my small way of striving to make a difference. I am deeply grateful to all of them, and it is my privilege to share a small portion of their stories and insights with you.

Let's meet these mentors briefly; we will also revisit each of them in their respective areas of expertise throughout the book. I have included longer biographies in Appendix D.

WILL ALLEN

Will Allen is an innovator and inventor with more than one hundred patents. His contributions, spanning groundbreaking technologies in physical printing to advancements in digital pathology, have left an indelible mark on major corporations like HP and Iron Mountain. For context, less than 1 percent of inventors throughout history have achieved this level of prolific success in IP creation.

Allen embodies a rare combination of curiosity, collaboration, and mentorship that has shaped transformative products and the careers of countless individuals. Within the first year of knowing him, I witnessed him stand up an entire patent process within a global organization. Among his many initiatives, he singlehandedly established a fast-track sustainability patent program that resulted in an international innovation contest, leading to several first-time inventors obtaining patents. With his work at Oregon State University, Allen inspires a new generation of innovators to create and lead with curiosity, purpose, and a commitment to building something greater than themselves.

KATHLEEN MORIARTY

Kathleen Moriarty is a visionary in the fields of technology and security, with her career rooted in the meticulous and high-impact world of standards development. She is a titan in her domain, having invented the "Real Time Internet Work Defense" protocol—the first of its kind for internet tracebacks and incident response. As a former area director for the Internet Engineering Task Force (IETF) and a current board member of the Internet Society (ISOC), Moriarty is instrumental in establishing critical standards that continue to protect users worldwide.

Moriarty is the founder of SecurityBiaS (Built-in at Scale), a groundbreaking company at the forefront of security innovation that combines open source code, standards, and intellectual property to redefine the future of technology and business. She has also served as the chief technology officer of the Center for Internet Security, where she further cemented her legacy as a leader in safeguarding digital systems through significant and unique thought leadership aimed at advancing security to better serve those with few resources. She is the author of *Transforming Information Security* and an adjunct faculty member at Georgetown University, where she teaches and inspires future generations of security experts.

STEVE TODD

Steve Todd redefines what it means to be prolific. He has had nearly three hundred patents granted, has authored two influential books, has published hundreds of blog posts and white papers, and has spoken at countless industry events—all while shaping critical conversations around data innovation and strategy. But Todd's impact extends far beyond this. As a Dell Technologies Fellow, he has translated visionary ideas into tangible intellectual property, driving hundreds of millions of dollars in revenue through customer adoption.

What makes Todd stand out is both the scale of his contributions and his ability to connect and collaborate. Todd's openness in sharing his insights and creative process has amplified his influence far beyond his own company. One of his many notable achievements is gaining approval to open source the Alvarium project, a feat that highlights his exceptional ability to navigate corporate politics and push forward innovation in even the most traditional environments.

ANNE-MARIE McREYNOLDS

Anne-Marie McReynolds is a trailblazer in community building and technology leadership whose impact extends far beyond her own achievements. From her start as an investigative journalist to a position of leadership at Dell, where she ran a global patent committee, McReynolds has crafted a formidable technology career while identifying opportunities to advance equity and empower others. She is an innovator with forty patents filed and also an impactful mentor, creating opportunities for underrepresented groups at a scale that is truly industry-changing.

McReynolds's leadership as a mentor in the US Department of State's TechWomen program exemplifies her ability to connect IP with social impact. Under her guidance, women from over fifteen countries have solved culturally significant problems and pitched their innovative ideas to venture capitalists, including Amazon Web Services. Most recently, she mentored a team of five Pakistani women who created the winning pitch—an AI-driven platform designed to support the sale of handcrafted goods, a project that is aimed to have a profound impact on the ability of local women to support their families. In Pakistan, four out of five women are unemployed, and 81 percent of artisans are home-based women. Through her mentorship, these women have secured seed funding to build solutions that make a tangible difference in their communities.

BILL PFEIFER

Bill Pfeifer is a master of connections and thought leadership, with a career defined by compelling stories that resonate across industries. As the host of a podcast on edge computing, Pfeifer brought together thought leaders from diverse domains, skillfully bridging technical insights with broader, relatable narratives. His storytelling doesn't just inform; it drives influence and action, creating real-world impact in ways few others achieve.

Despite his far-reaching impact, Pfeifer is characteristically modest, rejecting the label of "thought leader" and focusing instead on enabling others to shine. His collaborative approach and his ability to weave technical expertise into accessible, powerful narratives make him a force for positive change across industries. Pfeifer's work exemplifies the power of intellectual property when paired with storytelling, showcasing how connecting ideas and amplifying voices can drive innovation and elevate entire fields. Whether by identifying hidden potential, championing sustainability, or amplifying diverse voices, Pfeifer offers invaluable lessons in influence, strategy, and connection.

These leaders' stories and insights offer invaluable lessons for harnessing IP to drive industry influence and create lasting impact.

At the end of the day, this book is a roadmap for turning ideas into influence. Let's unlock those doors, share what we build, and change the game for those who follow. Your journey with IP starts now, and it's going to be extraordinary.

1

IP JOURNEYS

MY IP JOURNEY

As we explore IP in practice, it's essential to know that success with creating IP is rarely a straight line. For me, it was an evolving journey, a series of both intentional and accidental discoveries. My career started in the fast-paced world of startups where I published articles. Then, as I transitioned into midsize and global enterprises, I stumbled upon unexpected opportunities for more types of IP creation. These experiences taught me that even routine tasks can lay the groundwork for IP.

At the time of writing, I have fifty-eight granted utility patents and thirty-eight additional patents pending in the United States Patent and Trademark Office review process. This places me in the top 1 percent of inventors of all time by patent volume. Combined, I have published more than fifty articles, papers, and books. I've lost count of the videos, podcasts, and public speaking engagements I've done. If anyone had suggested to me twenty years ago that this would be the case, I would have shaken my head in disbelief. Conversely, if I'd had the knowledge of what I was doing or the frameworks of focus that I lay out for you in this book, these numbers would have been significantly higher.

Leveraging IP has opened countless doors for me that many don't realize are within their reach. This journey has connected me with incredible minds from all over the world. I've connected with friends and collaborators who share my passion for innovation and helped peers gain professional mobility.

Leveraging IP has also allowed me to build a career in which I choose the roles I want and advance initiatives that align with my personal values, such as advocating for AI ethics. My IP portfolio has given me the freedom to stand up for what I believe in, whether it's calling out injustices in the workplace or using my platform to mentor and empower underrepresented voices in technology.

By creating, protecting, and promoting your ideas, you gain the authority (and confidence) to push boundaries, explore new ventures, and, most importantly, stay true to who you are and what you stand for.

Early Stage: Startups and Accidental Discoveries

I am incredibly lucky. I entered the job market on the upswing of the dot-com boom of the late nineties, when unemployment was low and anyone with a software internship was employable. I landed a job at Connected Corporation. The company was building a software-as-a-service (SaaS) backup and recovery application, the first of its kind. Our founder and CEO was Dave Cane, a brilliant engineer who saw the opportunity to protect people's digital information. Cane's concept was simple: take the data on people's personal computers and make a copy of it hosted in a different location. The team built the tech and was awarded patents on how to store and recover data at scale. That IP (and Cane's credibility) created a moat protecting us from larger competitors, and the startup thrived.

In my early twenties, I was promoted to run one of the engineering teams; this promotion placed me literally at the table of engineering leadership. I was surrounded by architects who created patents and who were celebrated with stock options and gold-star paperweights. They had authority and recognition, and I am unashamed to admit that I wanted that, too. The only problem? I felt I wasn't at the technology forefront; I wasn't writing the sexy new code that got patented. Instead, I led the sustaining engineering team, fixing the things that went wrong and doing custom integrations. It didn't seem glamorous, but it was an essential role.

If only I had known then what I know now: customer problems provide copious opportunities to create a massive amount of IP. I missed so many IP opportunities.

LESSON LEARNED: DON'T WAIT—BUILD YOUR OWN CREDIBILITY

Early in my career, I focused on building connections inside my company, but I'd made a strategic mistake: I hadn't built any visibility outside of it. When I realized I needed to leave in order to grow, I didn't have a strong external network or any evidence that others should bet on me.

I thought patents were out of reach, even though I had the technical insight. What I did have was a writing degree, so I started small by publishing a technical article about win/loss analysis in Pragmatic Marketing's professional journal, *The Pragmatic Marketer*. It wasn't earth-shattering, but it solved a problem I understood well and it gave me something I could point to. Something that said: I know what I'm doing.

Around the same time, a director-level job opened up; I didn't apply since I assumed I wasn't qualified. I thought if I was qualified, someone would have reached out to me. When I talked to Cane after they gave someone else the position, he said something I've never forgotten: "You should never wait for someone to tell you to apply." That hit hard.

From then on, I stopped waiting. I applied for every job that looked exciting whether I was qualified or not. I kept writing. I built a portfolio of IP with articles and videos. I used social media to grow my reach. That platform-building gave me IP, which gave me external credibility, which in turn became my calling card: it got me speaking gigs, it got me job offers, it got me into rooms where decisions were made.

The real shift wasn't just the IP; it was learning to stop asking for permission and start building my own reputation.

Midstage: Medium-Sized Enterprises

Transitioning from startups to midsize enterprises brought a different set of challenges and a new understanding of what IP could be.

At a startup, IP was about standing out. But in midsize companies, I discovered something new: IP could bring people together. It could build community.

At Stratus, under the leadership of Ed Brennan, we were developing fault-tolerant cloud technology. IP wasn't a company priority; there were no incentives, no formal process. But Ed saw the potential. He proposed something bold: use patent creation as a team sport. We mapped out the customer and buyer journey together, found a novel insight worth protecting, and filed a team patent on using tags to identify the behaviors of virtual workloads in OpenStack.

That changed everything for me.

Until then, I had seen IP as individual proof, evidence that I knew what I was doing. This was different. It was collaborative, creative, and energizing. That patent became a shared win. And in the process, I learned how powerful IP could be for culture.

But in presenting it to our internal team, I made a mistake born from that "individual proof" mentality. I stood in front of the room and said things like, "I talked to fifty customers" and "I came up with this idea."

After the meeting, Brennan pulled me aside.

"If you're presenting something that represents the team," he said, "drop the word 'I.' Nothing will turn your team against you faster than taking credit for their work even if it's unintentional. Say 'we.'"

That moment stuck with me.

It was a simple shift. But it changed how I saw leadership, collaboration, and credit. When you give others visibility, you build trust. When you share IP creation, you grow influence together. That advice from Brennan has guided me for fifteen years. It's not about "I." It's about "we."

LESSON LEARNED: INNOVATE TOGETHER

At another medium-sized enterprise, Sepaton, I had a new opportunity to generate IP: a process improvement based on customer feedback. I'd spoken to dozens of users and learned that installing our hardware was frustrating. The instructions were dense, text-heavy, and hard to follow. We were using words to describe a physical, three-dimensional task. I knew this was an opportunity to create a community, so I teamed up with both our marketing teams and our User Experience (UX) teams to think *inside* the installation box.

Inspired by consumer technology (Apple's simple setup guides) we created a placard packed on top of the hardware. It showed, in one diagram, exactly how to wire the device. Installation times dropped from seventy minutes to under thirty. That single change became a copyrighted asset and one of my proudest examples of IP grounded in early design thinking. By creating that community with the UX team and including diverse skills, we started winning deals and accolades because of our usability.

Late Stage: Large Enterprises

As I moved into larger enterprises, a whole new power dynamic emerged, one where I was suddenly anonymous. The hierarchy was deep; I was just a number to decision-makers three levels above me. These leaders were making budget and strategy calls that affected thousands of employees, and they didn't know my name or the names of my teammates.

And here's a hard truth: it's easier to lay off people you've never met.

If I didn't take action, I knew I (and the people I cared about) would remain invisible, vulnerable to layoffs. That's when I remembered IP could help people stand out in a crowded room. It could shift perception, build credibility, and create upward momentum inside a massive organization.

LESSON LEARNED: INFLUENCE CHANGE

There's a saying that a rising tide lifts all boats. But in large enterprises, I learned something else: a rising tide drowns anyone not in a boat. And no one hands you a boat; you have to build it yourself. IP became my boat-building kit, and I started using it to help others build their boats too.

About six months into this job, a mentor invited me to an internal engineering summit. When I walked into the room, there were two hundred attendees, fewer than twenty of whom were women. Most were part of an elite technical community that required nominations and a mysterious vetting process. To an outsider, it felt like a secret society: badges, pins, invite-only meetings. But that invitation was a gift. It showed me exactly where I wanted to be.

With another mentor's guidance, I started navigating the system. I learned that most promotion criteria were subjective: things like "visibility" or "influence." But one thing wasn't subjective: IP. Patents and publications gave me numbers—proof—something that couldn't be dismissed or misinterpreted.

So, I asked questions. I met with patent committee members and inventors; I studied pass rates, funding models, and the company's strategic priorities; and I found out the average number of patents among this group. I decided I would double it. To be undeniably approved for membership, I'd need to have fifty patents (assuming the majority would be rejected) and more than a dozen papers, talks, and podcast appearances to back them up.

I spent the next year talking to customers, identifying problems, and spending my weekends filing disclosures. But from day one, I knew I didn't want to be the only one in the room who looked like me; I wanted others there, too. So I started evangelizing the "IP trick."

We formed groups called Patent Fun Time, where we mentored each other and filed patents together.

At first, my pass rate was low, but it improved; I began outperforming the average. Eventually, I became so efficient that people started coming to me with their ideas, asking for help turning them into patent disclosures. Within a year, more than ten women who participated in those mentoring circles were promoted or invited into that elite community. It was career-altering for all of us.

But influence isn't always easy.

Quite recently, I presented a patent submission to a review committee. One of the architects attacked me publicly, stating "You don't know what an invention is." His tone was dismissive, his three patents dated, and his behavior unprofessional. I was shocked, but I wasn't shaken. At the time of the incident, I had forty-nine granted patents in the prior four years. My portfolio spoke louder than his insult. Instead of shrinking, I stood up for my idea by reasserting the value of the patent and ignoring the personal attack.

And that's the difference.

Public IP is as close to objective as it gets in this industry: it's not opinion, it's evidence. Having objective metrics demonstrating that I knew what I was talking about gave me confidence, leverage, and a platform not just for myself, but for others.

That's what this phase of my career became: helping people build and get in the boat. Teaching them how to generate their own visibility and showing them that credibility doesn't have to be granted; it can be built.

From advocating for myself in the startup world, to creating shared wins in midsize companies, to lifting up others in large enterprises, IP has been the throughline. It turned uncertainty into clarity. Individual effort into team success. Invisible work into undeniable impact.

CREATING YOUR IP JOURNEY

With IP, it's easy to get caught up in the legal jargon, processes, and endless reviews. But keep reminding yourself that at the heart of it all is you—your ideas, passions, and drive to turn a thought into something tangible that changes not just your life but the lives of others around you. The IP you create is a way to

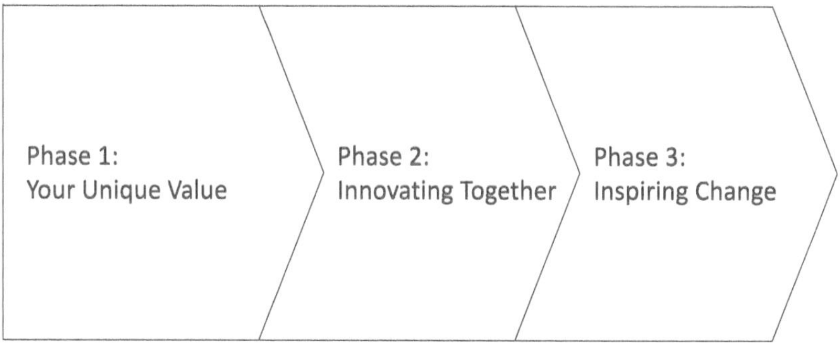

FIGURE 1.1 Phases of the IP journey. (Illustration by Nicole Reineke.)

achieve your goals. How you use it will evolve as you grow in your career.

Leveraging IP is a journey; your approach will mirror where you are in your professional growth, as figure 1.1 illustrates. When you start, IP may be about creating a credible foundation to express your expertise in a competitive environment. As you progress, it may become about collaboration and shared success. And at the later stage, you may choose to use your knowledge and influence to uplift others and transform industries. This journey from inventing to innovating to influencing is deeply personal, with IP as a thread weaving through every stage.

> IP gives you the opportunity to jump the line and gives you the power and control over your career to negotiate opportunity for yourself. For me, the patents we created allowed me to negotiate leadership. And then, I was given a budget of 200 patents a year. Now, how do I ensure we create those patents? I find and train rank-and-file people in the company.
>
> —ANNE-MARIE McREYNOLDS

For McReynolds, as she progressed, IP wasn't just about filing patents. It was about creating leverage, opening doors, and driving strategic growth across a community. Her experience bridges the three phases of IP creation laid out in figure I.1: inventing your unique value, innovating through collaboration, and using IP as a platform for influence.

In **Phase One: Your Unique Value**, I wrote articles to establish my credibility and land new opportunities. McReynolds used patents to establish her credibility and demonstrate her expertise. Filing patents helped her stand out, showcasing her ability to contribute meaningful and original ideas. This foundation of credibility provided her with the confidence and proof she needed to negotiate for leadership roles, showing that IP is a tangible way to articulate your unique value in a competitive environment.

Transitioning into **Phase Two: Innovating Together**, I started to build new community connections through team patents, standards committees, and coauthoring thought leadership. McReynolds moved beyond individual contributions to focus on empowering others. Her question, *"Where are those rank-and-file people in the company?"* highlights her commitment to democratizing innovation and ensuring that others have the opportunity to create their own IP. By mentoring colleagues and guiding them through the patent process, she fostered collaboration, built a sense of community, and created an environment where shared success was possible.

Finally, in **Phase Three: Inspiring Change**, I founded and currently lead a standards committee called the Consortium for AI Terminology for MSPs & IT Pros (CAT-MIP.org), teach courses at Georgetown University on AI Innovation, build mentor circles, speak at conferences, and lead AI at N-able. McReynolds's leadership allowed her to shape the direction of her organization's innovation strategy. With responsibility for a portfolio of 200 patents annually, she wasn't just advancing her career or her team. She was creating a systemic impact. By driving initiatives encouraging widespread participation in IP creation, McReynolds exemplified how IP can inspire change, influence industry trends, and leave a lasting legacy.

Our journeys show that IP is a tool for personal achievement and a framework for growth, collaboration, and transformation. It begins with defining your unique value, evolves into empowering others, and culminates in using your influence to shape the future of innovation. Each of these will be further explained in the next sections.

Phase One: Your Unique Value

It can be challenging to stand out when you're just starting your career, shifting directions, or embarking on your IP journey. The competition is fierce, and it often feels like your contributions get lost in the noise. Establishing a unique identity becomes crucial. You must show that you bring something fresh and valuable to the table to set you apart from others with similar skills or experience. IP can help you build credibility and external proof of value in a crowded market.

> When I started filing patents, it wasn't just about creating something new—it was about proving that I could contribute something meaningful that no one else had. Each invention became a tangible way to show my unique value, not just within my company but in the broader industry.
>
> —STEVE TODD

Early on, each patent was a technical achievement for Todd and a declaration of his unique value. Filing patents allowed him to demonstrate his expertise, creativity, and ability to solve problems in a way that stood out in his company and across the entire industry. It was his way of saying, "I'm here, and I have something important to contribute."

This mindset highlights the power of patents as a tool for building credibility and shaping a career. Each invention reflects your ability to think differently, push boundaries, and create something no one else has. Todd's quote reminds us that IP is about protecting ideas, carving out your space, making your mark, and showing the world what you can achieve.

For me, my first publication in *Pragmatic Marketing Magazine* wasn't just a technical accomplishment but a declaration of existence. It felt like I was shouting, "I am here; I have something to say!" IP is a tangible way to show that I am a creator, a thinker, and someone worth listening to. And in industries where it is hard to be seen in a crowd, IP can serve as a box to stand on.

Many people hope someone will notice their potential and open doors for them early on. But you have to push open those doors yourself. Publishing that first video or writing an article are ways of carving out your space in the industry. They say, "I want to make a difference here."

IP is a way to build mentorships and peer relationships in this stage. These connections are crucial because surviving in a corporate environment without friends or mentors can be challenging and, frankly, lonely. Working on IP—whether creating videos, writing articles, or just diving into new topics to fuel a budding idea—gives you a reason to reach out to others in your industry with specific questions. This is important for those of us who find networking awkward. Having clear, focused questions can help you find common ground, making it easier to build genuine relationships that support both personal and professional growth.

When you seek advice and assistance from collaborators, always give credit where credit is due; Ed Brennan's words to me ring true. Acknowledging those who contribute unique value to your work is not only the right thing to do but is essential to building lasting professional relationships. Many people, especially in competitive fields, fall into a scarcity mentality, fearing that sharing credit will diminish their contributions. Failing to recognize others' contributions is unethical and a fast track to damaging relationships and burning bridges. When you omit a contributor's name, you undermine trust, making future collaboration nearly impossible. Recognizing others doesn't take away from your success; it amplifies it. And in the long run, those relationships and mutual respect will open more doors than taking credit yourself ever could.

Phase Two: Innovating Together

As you establish yourself, the focus shifts from proving you individually exist to collaborating with others. In this stage, IP becomes more than just a personal achievement; it becomes a bridge to shared success. The goal is to create together to solve problems that matter to your team, customers, and community.

> I work across many different areas, finding ways to connect solutions from one domain to another. By combining expertise from different fields, we can reduce effort, relieve bottlenecks, and unlock progress that wouldn't have been possible alone.

> Collaboration gets more progress—you can do something you couldn't do before.
>
> —WILL ALLEN

By combining expertise from diverse fields, Allen focuses on reducing effort, solving bottlenecks, and unlocking new pathways for progress. His collaborative inventions are sitting in HP printers all over the world. This approach is all about using collaboration to amplify impact. It's solving a problem more efficiently and uncovering solutions that were previously out of reach. His perspective reminds us that the most exciting and transformative ideas often live at the edges where disciplines overlap.

Allen captures the essence of teamwork and shared knowledge. By embracing collaboration, we expand what's possible for ourselves and enable others to achieve things they couldn't do on their own. His insight reinforces the value of curiosity, connection, and the courage to explore new territory together. True innovation often happens in the spaces where ideas intersect. If you are sitting in a room alone or only exposed to the same group of people, you are missing an opportunity to think big.

Henry Chesbrough is another proponent of working with people outside your direct organization. His Open Innovation research emphasizes that real breakthroughs often come from looking outside your organization and embracing external contributions. His book *Open Innovation* is well worth reading if you are looking to collaborate and tap into a larger pool of ideas, accelerating the innovation process and making solutions that better meet market needs.

> I just want to play with brilliant people. And sometimes I'm surprised when they want to play with me.
>
> —BILL PFEIFER

At its heart, Pfeifer's statement reflects the thrill of working alongside talented, creative minds, people who challenge you, inspire you and push your thinking to places you couldn't reach alone. For Bill, "playing" with brilliant people isn't just about work; it's about the energy and excitement that comes from shared curiosity and innovation. It's the magic of exchanging ideas, testing theories, and building something bigger and better than any person could create on their own.

This phase requires a shift in mindset. It's not just about "What can I create and protect?" but "What can we create together?" It's about using your IP experience to work with and learn from others, where everyone can see opportunities they might have missed. By working with others, you will also find that your success grows.

Phase Three: Inspiring Change

At the highest level, IP becomes a platform for influence. This stage is where your focus shifts from collaboration to community. You want to think about how to use your hard-won expertise and authority to make a lasting impact in a way that is meaningful to you. You may wish to create direction in your company or even across an entire industry. IP is one way to uplift others, mentor the next generation, and drive long-term change. Inspiring change and influence does not require you to adopt TikTok and call yourself an influencer. That may be the path you choose, but the ultimate measure of your success is having the choice to impact the world in a way that aligns with who you are and your goals.

Influence takes many forms and is as unique as the person defining it. You are the only one who can determine what influence means for you. It's not about social media metrics or the size of your audience; it's about aligning your actions with your goals and values. Whether your influence comes from improving lives, leading groundbreaking projects, or setting new industry standards, the power lies in finding a path that resonates with who you are and the change you want to make. Influence is not one-size-fits-all; it's using your expertise and passion to make an impact that feels authentic to you.

> I am fortunate to have the opportunity to review proposals submitted to several major conferences in my area of expertise, which keeps me aware of current research. Work in standards typically operates at least three years ahead of the industry, providing additional valuable insight. Thought leadership gives me a platform to share these meaningful informed predictions, and having that insight builds trust with others.
>
> —KATHLEEN MORIARTY

Moriarty is one of my greatest mentors in influence. Her work as a founder, educator, standards leader, and contributor to significant conference committees demonstrates how thought leadership can be a powerful tool for shaping industries and driving meaningful change.

Her ability to see across different work streams and provide unique insights is a perfect example of how IP, combined with leadership, enables her to shape the broader conversation. She isn't following trends. She's helping to define them. Her focus is much wider than individual and collaborative achievements. Her work in securing technology through the Center for Internet Security and now SecurityBiaS is creating a lasting impact that benefits industries, communities, and future generations.

2

SPARKING IDEAS THAT BECOME IP

Before you can create IP, you need an idea—but not just any idea. You need one with the potential to grow, connect, and solve a meaningful problem. This chapter is about how to get there.

The most powerful ideas come from paying attention. They come from what you're learning, what frustrates you, and what others are trying to fix in their own way. They come from conversations that make you curious and from noticing when different fields are quietly struggling with the same thing.

The good news is that there is a repeatable, grounded process for finding ideas that matter. This section will guide you through finding ideas through problem discovery, how to evaluate problems, how to ideate on them, and what to do once the idea takes shape. One good idea can become a paper, a patent, a standard, a story, or a platform for much more.

IDEAS

The most common question everyone asks me is, "How do you come up with so many ideas?"

The short answer is that I'm always learning. I've built a strong foundation of expertise in technology, and I constantly connect everything I read, watch, and hear back to those areas of expertise. This approach helps me uncover opportunities for collaboration and innovation.

In the interviews I conducted for this book, my mentors revealed their own unique spins on this strategy, whether intentionally or accidentally.

> I visualize this as cartoons, where two cartoon characters can grab each other and lift their chairs, and they both go up. Ideas are like that. You and I can have ideas together right now. It floats us all up. You're never out of ideas—it's not a zero-sum game.
>
> —WILL ALLEN

You can see here why Allen is one of my favorite collaborators. He captures something compelling about collaboration and creativity.

Think of it this way: in his metaphor, the cartoon characters lifting each other represent what happens when we share ideas and collaborate. Just like those characters defying logic and rising together, ideas build on one another, creating an upward momentum. This isn't a zero-sum game where one person's gain is another's loss. Instead, creativity is infinite. When you contribute an idea, it sparks more ideas, and everyone involved rises higher together.

What makes this perspective so meaningful is how it reframes collaboration. It's not about protecting your ideas or worrying about losing credit; it's about embracing the co-creation process and recognizing that shared effort makes the whole greater than the sum of its parts. Allen's visualization reminds us that the best ideas don't happen in isolation; they're born in connection and shared curiosity, lifting everyone to new heights.

> I started reflecting on my own innovation approach, which I called innovation by adjacency. I became an expert in certain software fields by writing code and shipping a product, and then I learned about an adjacent technology that could be combined with what I already knew. Combining prior knowledge with something new led to the 'aha' moments that became immediate invention disclosures.
>
> —STEVE TODD

When Steve Todd talks about innovation by adjacency, he's describing a brilliant strategy for generating fresh ideas and breakthroughs. His method is grounded in building expertise in a particular area and deliberately exploring adjacent technologies or fields to discover new opportunities. The resulting "aha" moments are clear and compelling ideas that are immediately ready to be documented as invention disclosures.

What's so powerful about this approach is how it transforms incremental learning and conversations with peers into exponential innovation. Todd isn't starting from scratch with each new idea; he's leveraging his deep foundation of knowledge and looking for connections that others might overlook. It's a reminder that innovation doesn't always come from diving into the unknown. It often happens at the edges of our understanding, where our expertise intersects with new perspectives or technologies.

This approach is something we can all adopt. Whether in software, design, or any field, think about the spaces adjacent to your expertise. What's happening just outside your current focus? Who is working in areas that overlap with your skills? Combining what you know with what's new opens the door to endless possibilities for growth and creativity. Todd's method is a practical and repeatable way to create impactful ideas, one adjacency at a time.

> The things that I've gained from [talking to experts from different fields] have been huge—most of it is just perspective and the ability to connect different ideas. For example, I had a conversation about the space-based economy and later tied it into discussions on data centers in space. It's about jumping outside of my comfort space and helping others jump outside theirs to explore new possibilities.
>
> —BILL PFEIFER

Pfeifer's approach highlights the importance of curiosity and connection. The ideas of a space-based economy and data centers might seem unrelated at first but, when connected, spark entirely new possibilities. This kind of cross-disciplinary thinking drives innovation and allows us to see challenges and solutions in ways others might not.

The real magic in Pfeifer's method is how it invites others to do the same: by encouraging people to explore outside their usual boundaries, he creates an environment where everyone can think bigger and more creatively. Pfeifer's quote reminds us that growth and innovation often come from the intersections of ideas, where different perspectives collide and create something entirely new. We should look beyond what we know and embrace the potential of what could be.

IP Idea Methodologies in Action

How do I apply these? Let me share an example of a nascent (and likely to be debunked) IP project I'm working on.

Recently, my son started an electrical engineering degree, getting exposure to tools that measure and produce electromagnetic fields. As he shared what he was learning, our conversation took a turn into how he could "test" out his design ideas with AI-created synthetic personas, a field of research I am working on. Synthetic personas are an idea in AI-driven user experience research, where detailed data from interviews and observed and measured behavior from end users can be ingested into generative AI to create new, synthesized representations of how a person may act in a situation. These personas can even interact in ways that align with their synthesized traits, offering a powerful way to refine interview techniques and ensure you're asking the right questions to elicit meaningful insights prior to high-cost interactions with real people.

Synthetic personas typically represent an archetype but don't have to be limited to humans. In theory, you could create a synthetic representation of anything: a plant, an animal, or even an inanimate object—perhaps even of an electronic device with a unique electromagnetic signature. That's when the light bulb went off. We stumbled upon an idea: could we augment synthetic personas to include electromagnetic signatures? Today, they are typically limited to text, voice, and video—could we extend the data types associated with these interactions to include electromagnetic fields? This is the basis of our current project.

This example shows how the intersection of three fields (AI, UX research, and electrical engineering) can spark an entirely new idea and way of thinking.

Here is where IP strategy can come in. Here is where IP strategy comes in. We can leverage this one idea into an IP portfolio (figure 2.1).

We can leverage this one idea into an IP portfolio. This idea can inform papers, conference topics, patents, standards participation, open source, or even register a company, and we can take

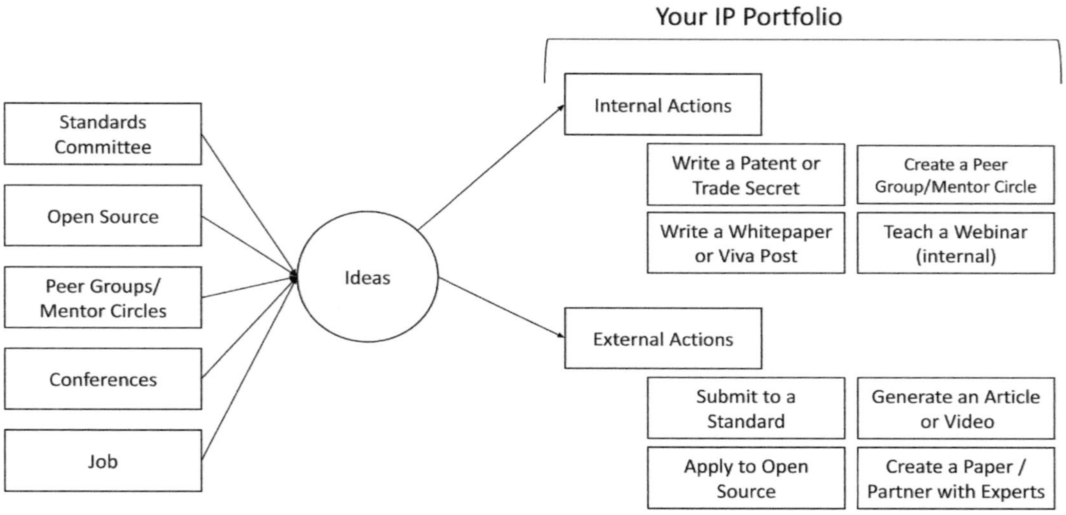

FIGURE 2.1 Turning ideas into IP. (Illustration by Nicole Reineke.)

internal actions such as pursuing the idea with trademarks and trade secrets opportunities. And there you have it: a car ride conversation transformed into limitless possibilities for IP.

You may notice that I said I will turn this idea into a portfolio; portfolio thinking is a foundational concept for leveraging IP. I do not just say that this is a patent: inventions, articles, books, art, standards, code, designs, logos, and brand names all fall under the umbrella of IP. IP is how we legally protect those creations. Each serves a different purpose, offering unique ways to secure recognition or financial rewards for what you've invented or created. A portfolio is building up the set of content to derive personal impact.

TURNING IDEAS INTO IP

You must broaden your view of what you work on to consider how you can flip ideas into a portfolio that will impact where you are and support your career growth. A portfolio is a set of interconnected actions that collectively push an idea forward or solve a problem. These can be work assignments, like running a marketing campaign, designing a solution to a technical issue, or self-initiated side projects driven by your interests or expertise. The power of portfolios lies in their potential to produce multiple outcomes from a single stream of effort. With thoughtful planning, one idea can lead to various valuable results, multiplying its impact.

This principle is well-illustrated in marketing, which often focuses on repurposing content. For example, start with one high-value piece of long-form content, such as a whitepaper or video. By breaking it down and reformatting it, you can create 20 or more new pieces of content like blog posts, social media clips, infographics, podcast episodes, and more. This strategy ensures that the effort invested in creating the original content has a broader reach and longer lifespan.

Gary Vaynerchuk (Gary Vee) in his book, *Day Trading Attention*, emphasizes this approach in his philosophy of "content creation at scale." He advocates starting with a cornerstone piece of content, like a keynote speech or a comprehensive blog post, and then slicing and dicing it into smaller, bite-sized pieces for different platforms. According to him, each piece should be optimized for its shared medium, ensuring it resonates with the audience. For example, a longer-form LinkedIn article could become a series of tweets, a short Instagram reel, or a one-minute video. The goal is to maximize the value of your work by meeting your audience wherever they are, in formats they prefer, all while staying true to your original message. This isn't a prescription for engineers to start running marketing campaigns (though that may be an interesting idea), but rather a way for you to rethink the number and types of outcomes you generate when you are working on a problem.

Applying this mindset to your IP means thinking strategically about how each action or outcome can be leveraged in multiple ways. While working on your ideas, consider building assets that can be repurposed, shared, and scaled to amplify your results. Whether working on a professional assignment or a passion project, this approach can transform your efforts into a platform for more significant influence and success.

We know a portfolio mindset is essential, but which ideas and projects should you work on?

> I've always viewed project selection as a win-win-win. When you choose something aligned with your expertise, involve others, and take risks, you multiply the impact—mentoring others, advancing your ideas, and driving value for the company.
>
> —STEVE TODD

Todd emphasizes the power of alignment, collaboration, and bold thinking. Choosing the right project is solving a problem, finding the sweet spot where your skills shine, your colleagues bring their strengths, and the community benefits from innovative outcomes. Todd sees project selection as an opportunity to create ripples: advancing your personal growth, empowering others, and delivering tangible value to the organization.

A critical element in achieving this "win-win-win" is understanding what your company or community values most. Every organization has strategic priorities, and aligning your projects with these ensures they will be supported and impactful. Whether it's driving revenue, improving customer experiences, or enhancing operational efficiency, knowing what the company aims to achieve allows you to choose projects that resonate with leadership goals. This alignment increases the chances of your project's success and elevates your visibility and influence within the organization, reinforcing your role as a trusted contributor and innovator.

To align your projects with your company's goals, you must have a solid grasp of your business strategy. But what does knowing your company's strategy mean, and how can you use this knowledge to make impactful project decisions?

Knowing

Knowing your business strategy means understanding your organization's overarching goals and objectives. Every company has a mission and priorities, whether explicitly stated or implied through its actions. These priorities can include increasing revenue, expanding market share, enhancing customer satisfaction, driving innovation, or reducing costs. Identifying what matters most to your company allows you to position your projects as solutions to these high-level goals.

Start by asking: What are the top three objectives my organization is trying to achieve this year? Leadership announcements, public filings, quarterly updates, or internal communications often outline these priorities. For example, if the company aims to enhance customer experience, look for metrics like Net Promoter Score (NPS) or customer retention rates as key indicators of success. If innovation is a priority, focus on initiatives that foster creative solutions or bring new products to market faster.

Once you know the broader goals, drill down into the success metrics. Does your organization define Key Performance Indicators (KPIs)? KPIs are quantifiable markers that show progress toward these goals. For instance, sales growth or average deal size might be the key metrics in a revenue-driven strategy. For a company focusing on operational efficiency, KPIs could include cost savings, process improvements, or time-to-delivery reductions. Business indicators often operate on a higher level, providing insight into company health and performance, such as profit margins, employee engagement, or market positioning.

When you understand the company's strategic priorities and how success is measured, you can ensure your projects directly contribute to these goals. For example, if your organization prioritizes customer retention, a project to streamline onboarding processes or reduce customer service response times will resonate. If the company is driving innovation, focus on initiatives that expand IP creation or enhance product capabilities. It will be a good thing for your career if your projects support revenue growth—it can make it easier to justify your paycheck and avoid being in the next round of layoffs.

Forging Connections

Connecting your work to what matters most to the organization is key.

> I figured out you need to do good work, and people need to appreciate it and understand why it's happening . . . I started by focusing on one project at a time, going deep into it, and learning everything I could to make a meaningful impact before moving on to the next thing.
>
> —WILL ALLEN

Allen's approach perfectly complements this idea. Allen emphasizes that good work must not only be done but also be understood and appreciated. By dedicating himself to each project, he ensures that the outcomes are impactful and resonate with stakeholders and organizational goals.

This connection between alignment and depth is critical. When you focus on projects that align with strategic priorities and execute them with thoroughness, you create work that solves problems and builds credibility. Your contributions are seen as intentional, thoughtful, and deeply tied to the company's success, amplifying your influence and positioning you as a trusted, high-impact contributor.

> I focus on areas where my expertise can make the most difference, particularly in standards development. By addressing critical gaps in security and ensuring interoperability, I can

contribute to projects that have both immediate and long-term impact.

—KATHLEEN MORIARTY

Moriarty highlights the importance of focusing your expertise on areas where you can create the most significant impact. When she says, *"I focus on areas where my expertise can make the most difference, particularly in standards development,"* she emphasizes the value of aligning your skills with organizational needs to address critical gaps and drive meaningful outcomes. In Moriarty's case, as the founder of SecurityBiaS, this helps her shape the business strategy. Her ability to address both immediate challenges and long-term goals demonstrates the power of intentional focus.

When you identify where your strengths align with your organization's goals and mission, you maximize the value of your work. Whether refining internal processes or shaping the future through industry standards, focusing on high-impact opportunities ensures your contributions resonate with stakeholders and create lasting success. Moriarty's approach shows how intentional alignment can elevate your work and establish you as a massive needle-mover in an industry.

Knowing your company's strategy also lets you better articulate your projects' value to stakeholders. When you can clearly explain how your work supports the business's top priorities and demonstrates alignment with KPIs, you increase buy-in and elevate the perceived importance of your contributions. This positions your projects for success and reinforces your role as a forward-thinking leader who understands and supports the company's vision.

Once you know the general direction and projects of high value to you and your company, you can start picking better ideas and breaking the larger research or outcomes into IP.

COME UP WITH IDEAS BY FINDING PROBLEMS

> A problem well-stated is a problem half-solved.
>
> —JOHN DEWEY

If you're wondering how to generate impactful IP, start here: look for problems.

Every innovation begins with a challenge worth solving. The more precisely you define the issue, the stronger your foundation for meaningful IP. In my experience across hundreds of patents, articles, and standards contributions, the most successful ideas all started with a moment of clarity about a real, pressing problem.

Whether it's a gap in cloud reliability, a bottleneck in manufacturing, or a limitation in space communication, problems are the sparks that ignite IP creation. Your job is to notice them. Stay curious, listen carefully, and think creatively about solutions that don't yet exist.

Finding and (sometimes) solving real problems creates real value, and IP is your way of documenting and defending that value.

Real Examples: Turning Problems into IP

Let's look at a few practical examples, each grounded in a challenge that needed a solution. These stories span industries and stages of development, and they all started the same way: with a well-defined problem.

EXAMPLE 1: MAKING THE CLOUD FAULT-TOLERANT

At a time when enterprise applications were just starting to move to the cloud, we saw a major risk: downtime during cloud server failures or demand spikes could cripple businesses.

To address this, my team built a system to monitor cloud environments in real time and automatically trigger failover mechanisms. The architecture, algorithms, and use cases were all documented for a patent disclosure—but they were also contributed to OpenStack standards, published in articles, and drove industry conversations. That particular patent wasn't granted, but the innovation was implemented and widely adopted. It also became a key piece of my credibility portfolio.

Takeaway: Even if a patent isn't granted, IP built on solving a high-impact problem can fuel reputation, adoption, and future opportunity.

EXAMPLE 2: COMMUNICATING IN DEEP SPACE

A colleague and I started exploring a fundamental constraint in space exploration: traditional radio signals degrade over long distances. That makes real-time communication with deep-space probes difficult and unreliable.

We envisioned using terahertz (THz) networks to boost signal speed and integrity. We didn't have access to the hardware or the resources to test it, but we documented the concept and laid out an implementation path; that disclosure resulted in a granted patent. That was proof that a well-defined problem and a compelling, novel approach can be enough, even without a prototype.

Takeaway: You don't have to build the solution yourself if you define the problem clearly and explain how someone skilled in the field could make it real. That can be enough for IP.

EXAMPLE 3: SCALING A SOURDOUGH FACTORY

In a completely different industry, my father-in-law, Johannes Reineke, ran a family sourdough bread business. They were losing time and product due to how traditional starter batches were handled: make a batch, use it, stop the process, and start again.

He solved this by inventing a continuous starter extraction process that kept fermentation going without the need to restart production. His design eliminated downtime, reduced waste, and was granted a patent. That innovation ended up in baking textbooks and played a role in his family's immigration application.

Takeaway: IP doesn't have to be technical to be transformative. If it solves a tangible problem and improves efficiency or outcomes, it's worth protecting.

THE COMMON THREAD: FIND A PROBLEM WORTH SOLVING

What ties all these stories together is clarity. Each started with a defined problem that was measurable, observable, and worth solving. The solution didn't need to be fully built. It needed to be plausible, purposeful, and described in enough detail that someone else could build it.

That's the real first step of creating IP.

Before you write an article, file a disclosure, or submit a patent, make sure you understand the problem you're solving and why it matters. That's what gives your work weight, whether it becomes a product, a publication, or an industry standard.

How to Spot Great Problems

Finding the right problems to solve is a skill. And like any skill, it improves with intention and practice.

Start by paying attention to what is broken, inefficient, frustrating, or just barely good enough in your day-to-day work. Every complaint is a clue. Every workaround is a signal. Don't overlook the small annoyances. Many great innovations come

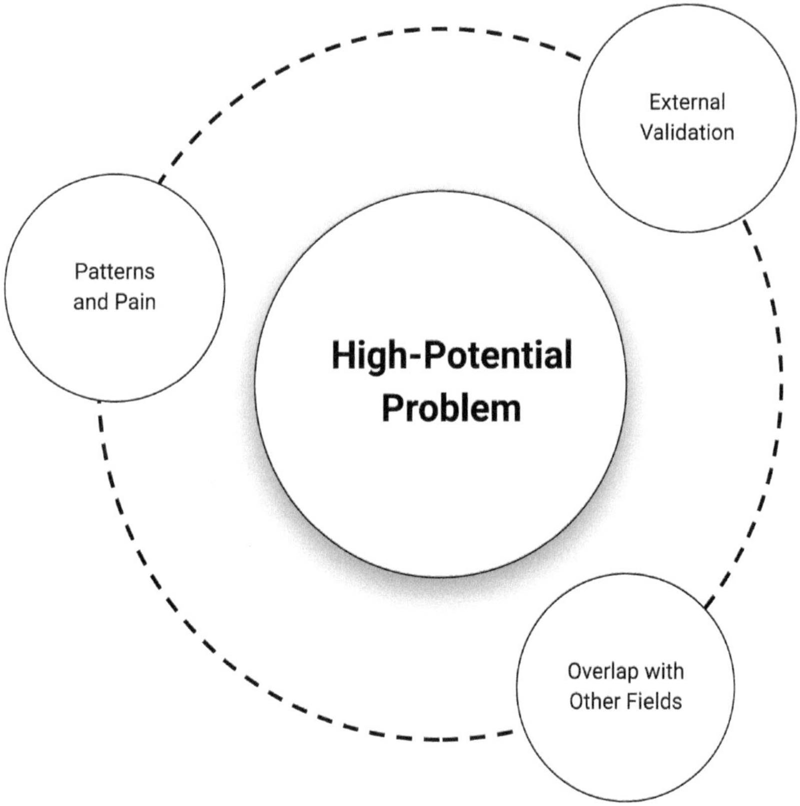

FIGURE 2.2 The makeup of a high-potential problem.
(Illustration by Nicole Reineke.)

from solving something that people assumed was just the way it is. These are inklings of what could be high-potential problems (figure 2.2).

One of the most powerful techniques to find problems is pattern recognition across conversations. Talk to customers, peers, or frontline users and listen for the same pain point showing up in different words. If you hear the same frustration more than once, write it down. That is a strong indicator you are onto something worth investigating.

Another method is to study edge cases, the situations where a process or system fails. Extreme use cases often expose assumptions or weaknesses in design. Ask questions like: What happens when this breaks? Where does it slow down under pressure? How does it behave when used in a completely unexpected way?

Some of the best problems to solve appear when you step outside your discipline; talking to people in different domains exposes you to challenges you would never find on your own. Often, different fields are wrestling with remarkably similar issues but use different language to describe them.

If you are in engineering, talk to people in operations, design, marketing, or legal. Ask them about their biggest friction points. Where do they spend more time than they want to? What tasks feel tedious or repetitive? What do they wish worked better?

This kind of cross-functional conversation helps you spot universal patterns, such as data overload, decision bottlenecks, poor handoffs, or tools that don't align with workflow needs. These patterns are often hiding in plain sight and can unlock opportunities for innovations that translate across teams and industries.

If you are feeling stuck, run a problem-finding sprint. Line up 15-minute conversations with three people from completely different backgrounds. Ask them the same three questions: What frustrates you about your work? Where do things break down? What would make your job easier? You might be surprised at the insights that surface.

The more perspectives you gather, the sharper your ability becomes to identify common threads and propose solutions that resonate widely. This is also how you build inclusive innovation, grounded in a diverse understanding of real-world problems.

Evaluating Problems Using a Framework

Once you've identified a list of promising problems (whether through your current job, personal interests, or side projects) you'll need a way to evaluate which ones are worth pursuing. A structured framework (figure 2.3) can help you assess four key dimensions: problem scope, data availability, business value, and risk.

By using this framework, you can prioritize ideas that are not only high value, but also aligned with your goals and likely to succeed.

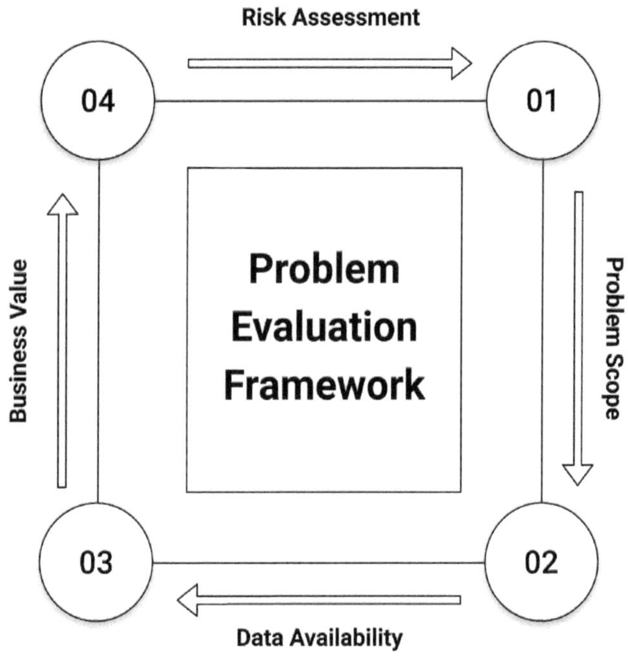

FIGURE 2.3 The problem evaluation framework. (Illustration by Nicole Reineke.)

1. PROBLEM SCOPE

Start by examining the effort currently required to achieve the outcome your project aims to improve or replace. You are looking for friction—anywhere people are losing time, accuracy, or sanity. Ask yourself:

- How much time and effort are spent on this task or process today?
- Are there repetitive, error-prone, or manual steps?
- What are the tangible pain points or operational risks?

For example, in one customer onboarding project, the existing process required manual approvals and data entry across four systems. It took days, sometimes weeks. By identifying this friction, the team saw an opportunity to automate data flow, streamline approvals, and reduce the cycle to under an hour.

Understanding where time is lost or failures occur gives you a baseline. This is what you'll use to justify your solution and measure its success.

2. DATA AVAILABILITY

If your idea involves automation, AI, or analytics, data is your raw material. But, we can also consider this from the perspective of anecdotal data and your access to information regarding the area. Evaluating data early helps you choose an approach that is both feasible and impactful.

Start with these questions:

- Do I have access to data that reflects the problem?
- Do I have customer feedback that indicates this is a real issue?
- Are there gaps in what I understand? If so, can I fill them with synthetic data or proxies?

Scenarios vary:

- Minimal Data: When proposing terahertz data transmission, we lacked real-world test data. So, we documented the inputs we would eventually need, along with models to simulate outcomes.
- Moderate Data: In a network optimization project, we had logs from active systems but needed to clean and structure the data before using it.
- Extensive Data: A telemetry-based AI feature we developed drew on millions of operational records. This made it ideal for building a predictive model with high confidence.

If you're missing real-world data, synthetic data may be helpful, but only if it's validated regularly. In fields like healthcare or finance, bias in synthetic data can lead to significant risks. Always confirm your assumptions.

3. BUSINESS VALUE

Not all good ideas are valuable in a business context. But if your goal is to advance your career through intellectual property, then business value matters. It helps justify resources, gain support, and increase the impact of your work.

Ask yourself:

- Will solving this problem save time, reduce costs, or improve reliability?
- Does it align with key goals like customer satisfaction, product quality, or market leadership?
- Could it differentiate your company and *you* from competitors?

Example:

A digital health startup identified a lag in getting updated data from wearable devices. By solving that problem, they cut syncing time by 85 percent and improved clinical outcomes. That solution became a patent, a case study, and a platform for new features.

Not every project will have a clear ROI at the start. But if you can link your idea to a known metric like churn reduction, increased NPS, or cost avoidance, it becomes much easier to get internal backing and to claim ownership of the outcome.

4. RISK ASSESSMENT

Every problem has risks. The goal is to identify them early and build strategies to manage them. Solving problems that put you into high-risk territory may be a double-edged sword.

Consider these dimensions:

- Implementation Risk: Do you have the skills, tools, and support to make the solution work? Will it perform reliably?
- Outcome Risk: What happens if it fails? Could it impact customers, expose private data, or create compliance issues?
- Reputational Risk: Are you overpromising, or working in a field with high scrutiny?

Example:

In a data-driven project for regulatory compliance, the team ran tabletop simulations to test what would happen if the model failed or made a biased recommendation. This helped build trust with leadership, who saw that risks were taken seriously and mitigations were in place.

Involving cross-functional teams, especially legal, compliance, or data privacy, early in your problem definition gives you better insight into risks and usually improves the outcome. Invite skeptics into the conversation. Their pushback helps strengthen your case and reduce blind spots.

(HONORARY) 5. JOY

This is not part of the formal framework, but I contest that you need to have a spark of interest and excitement when researching problems. A problem that connects with you personally makes the entire process more engaging and helps with the toil.

This framework of problem scope, data availability, business value, and risk is a practical filter. It helps you focus your effort on the problems that will create the most meaningful IP and demonstrate your ability to innovate with purpose.

You don't need to score perfectly in every category, but by evaluating your ideas systematically, you increase your odds of creating something valuable, defensible, and career-changing.

The goal is to pursue IP with intention, and that starts by choosing the right problem to solve. You can start to publish and give talks once you identify a problem or research area even if you do not have a solution to recommend. This can be useful in creating awareness of an issue and helping to form a group of people to swarm the problem. For some forms of IP, such as patents and trade secrets, you will need to take it a step further and find ways to solve the problem.

Solving Problems Using a Framework

Ironically, problem solving doesn't start with a solution. It starts with choosing a worthwhile problem and then approaching it with discipline and creativity. Once you've selected the right challenge, a structured problem-solving framework will help you turn insight into innovation and meaningful IP.

Here's a six-step framework I've used repeatedly to move from a problem to valuable, protectable IP.

Build a Diverse Team → Research State of the Art → Engage the Market → ID Key Challenges → Generate Solutions → Iterate and Refine

BRING TOGETHER A DIVERSE TEAM

Assemble a cross-functional team with a range of expertise, perspectives, and lived experiences. Great innovation comes from challenging assumptions, connecting dots others don't see, and exploring different ways of thinking.

> It's about connecting dots no one else has thought to connect.
>
> —WILL ALLEN

Invite people from different disciplines to the table. Diversity in role, background, and thinking style leads to unexpected breakthroughs. It also helps reduce blind spots and build stronger solutions from the start.

Try this: Bring together at least one person each from quality assurance, customer support, and sales teams for your next ideation session. Ask: *What's one problem you've had to solve this month that no one else seems to notice?*

RESEARCH THE STATE OF THE ART

Before designing a solution, immerse yourself in what already exists: look at everything from academic research product offerings, to open-source projects. This helps you avoid reinvention, identify gaps, and ensure your work pushes the field forward.

> Teaching them how to hustle and realize what exists today, and then add embodiments on top of it, creates opportunities for innovation.
>
> —ANNE-MARIE McREYNOLDS

Explore multiple sources:

- Academic: Google Scholar, IEEE, PubMed
- Industry: Gartner, McKinsey, Forrester, whitepapers
- Standards: Join or observe committees shaping your space
- Competitors: Analyze patents, product features, customer feedback
- Open Source: GitHub repositories and standard projects
- Conferences: Attend demos, workshops, and talks

Researching the state of the art is not a one-time activity; it's a continuous process that fuels creativity and strategic thinking. By thoroughly exploring academic publications, industry trends, and expert insights, you position your innovation within a well-informed context. This process helps you identify gaps and ensures your work builds on the strengths of what already exists, creating genuinely novel solutions. Great innovation starts with great research.

> By participating in standards and attending conferences, I gain insight that's often three or more years ahead of the industry.
>
> — KATHLEEN MORIARTY

Try this: Choose one market research report and one open-source project related to your field. Identify one gap and ask: *What's missing, and why hasn't it been solved yet?*

ENGAGE THE MARKET

Real problems live with real people. Talk to users, customers, and adjacent industry experts. Ask open-ended questions that uncover daily frustrations, workarounds, and unmet needs.

> If you ask the right questions and listen closely, people will give you the breadcrumbs. They'll uncover their story, pain points, and what matters to them.
>
> —BILL PFEIFER

Engaging the market is more than gathering data. You want to build genuine connections with potential users, ask the right questions, and uncover their deeper challenges. This step is critical because the best solutions start with an intimate understanding of real-world problems.

When you approach users or customers, avoid asking questions that imply a specific answer. Instead, use open-ended inquiries that allow them to share their experiences freely. For example:

- "Can you walk me through your biggest challenges when using this technology?"
- "What are the most time-consuming or frustrating parts of your current process?"
- "If you could wave a magic wand and fix one thing, what would it be?"

These kinds of questions uncover insights that might not surface otherwise. Listening carefully and allowing the conversation to flow naturally ensures you gather unfiltered, authentic feedback.

Sometimes, the best insights come from unexpected places. Bill Pfeifer's approach to engaging experts across disciplines exemplifies this idea.

> The podcast is about edge computing, but we've talked to people in AI, digital farming, and even the space-based economy. Tying

> it all back to edge computing shows how connections across fields lead to new perspectives.
>
> —BILL PFEIFER

This philosophy of market engagement means looking beyond immediate stakeholders. Consider talking to industry experts and researchers in adjacent fields. These conversations can reveal new angles or spark ideas that wouldn't have emerged in siloed discussions.

Try this: Interview three people who have the problem you are thinking about.

IDENTIFY KEY CHALLENGES

Once you've gathered raw insights, prioritize the real problems. Set aside assumptions. Use tools like journey mapping to surface systemic inefficiencies and emotional friction points.

How to make a journey map:

- Define the user and goal: Start by choosing a specific user persona and the task or experience you want to map (e.g., onboarding a new customer, handling a support request).
- Outline the steps: Break the journey into key stages or actions the user takes. Capture what they're doing, thinking, and feeling at each step.
- Identify pain points and gaps: Look for friction, delays, handoffs, or confusion. Highlight where users struggle, give up, or create workarounds.

Journey maps help you visualize a process, highlight failure points, and locate high-impact opportunities. In one project focused on fault-tolerant infrastructure, mapping revealed that IT teams spent hours managing manual failovers. That insight led to an automated solution that significantly reduced downtime.

At this stage, one of the biggest risks is assuming you already know the answers. It's easy to fall into the trap of interpreting user feedback through the lens of your existing knowledge or experience. However, this can close your eyes to the real issues that need attention. Instead, approach the data with an open mind. Treat every piece of feedback as a clue, not a conclusion, and allow the challenges to emerge organically.

Steve Todd's approach to *"innovation by adjacency"* can be a helpful mindset here. This ability to connect challenges from one area with solutions from another can help you uncover opportunities that others might miss.

Try this: Create a journey map for one user scenario. Highlight where people struggle, delay, or improvise. These are high-leverage opportunities for innovation. Before moving forward, validate your journey map with one or more users.

GENERATE A BROAD RANGE OF SOLUTIONS

Once the challenges are clear, the next step is brainstorming solutions. Encourage your team to think big and generate a range of ideas. Some might seem wildly ambitious, while others may feel more grounded. The key is to balance idealism with practicality, ensuring the solutions are innovative and implementable.

A solution is only as powerful as your ability to convey it.

Start with storyboards or narratives. Show how your idea changes the user experience. Use visuals, timelines, or simple sketches to communicate your vision clearly.

Try this: For each challenge you identified, generate three solution ideas: one simple, one ambitious, and one unexpected. Sketch the user flow for each. AI tools like Vo.dev, Figma, even ChatGPT are exceptional at helping produce these artifacts.

ITERATE AND REFINE

Even the best ideas need polish. Share early prototypes, narratives, or system diagrams with users and stakeholders. Get feedback early and often. Use that input to refine your approach, adjust your assumptions, and sharpen your IP story.

Don't wait for perfection. Focus on clarity, feasibility, and impact.

Try this: Present your idea to a peer and ask them to tell the story back to you. If they can explain it clearly and with enthusiasm, you're on the right track.

Following this framework grounds your innovation in real problems, aligns your work with what matters most, and ensures the solution is deeply informed, testable, and defensible.

Those who want more structure can explore additional frameworks for challenge mapping, interviews, storyboarding, and IP planning discussed in *Compassion-Driven Innovation.*

Innovation is not just inspiration. It's a process and it drives your IP.

Now that you know what problems you will be approaching and how you may solve them, lets dive into how you create your IP.

3

IP IN DEPTH

IP is a toolbox. This chapter is designed to show you what's possible and give you a practical way in. We'll cover what each type of IP protects, why it matters, and how to get started.

One of the keys to knowing how to use IP is understanding what each tool is designed to do, so we'll walk through six core types of IP: patents, trade secrets, copyrights, trademarks, open-source contributions, and standards. You'll learn how each works, how to create them, and how to decide which one best matches your skills, your ideas, and your goals.

Traditionally, conversations around IP focus on patents, trademarks, and copyrights. But to build a visible and credible portfolio in today's world, you need a broader view. Open source and standards are equally powerful forms of IP—especially when you're looking to grow your career, elevate your reputation, or create evidence of your expertise in environments where traditional IP isn't always accessible.

Your experience and expertise will influence the type of IP you create. Starting with what feels natural to you can make all the difference. Early in my career, I lacked the confidence to pursue patents. At the time, I assumed patents were only for people who had mastered a specific technical field or worked in cutting-edge innovation labs. Looking back, I realize this hesitation stemmed from a lack of education and exposure, and I wish I hadn't let it hold me back. You should not let it hold you back. If you are still unsure, consider that someone was granted patent US6871616B2—a pet umbrella (figure 3.1).

You don't need to create every form of IP—but knowing each type and how it works will help you make informed, strategic choices about how you pursue IP in your portfolio.

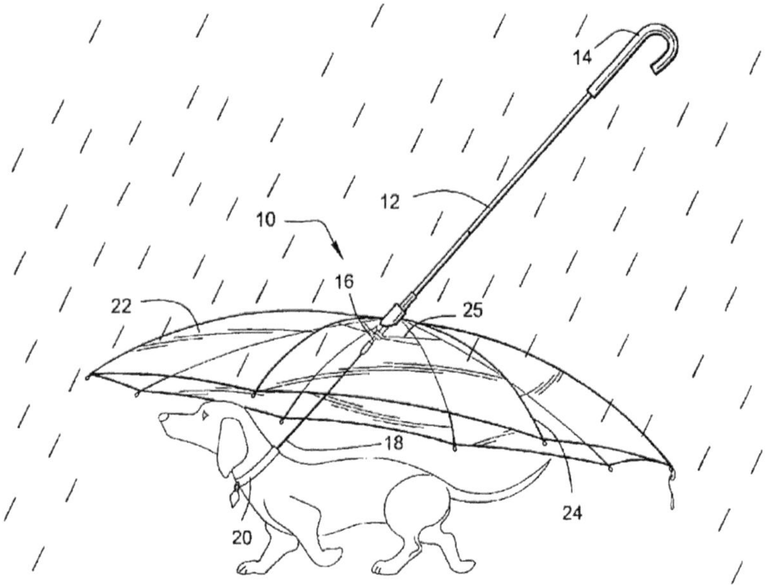

FIGURE 3.1 Image from *Pet Umbrella and Combined Pet Leash and Umbrella*, patent US6871616B2, granted to Irina Zhadan-Milligan and Yuri Zhadan in 2005.

IP TYPES

Patents

Patents protect inventions, giving creators exclusive rights for a set period. This can include, for example:

- Pharmaceutical drug formulas—such as the chemical composition of new medications
- Software-related inventions—like algorithms or processes solving complex problems
- Product designs—the aesthetic features that define modern devices
- Medical devices—innovative surgical tools or diagnostic equipment
- Electric vehicle advancements—including new battery technologies or charging methods
- Plants—new, distinct plant varieties, such as disease-resistant crops or uniquely colored flowers

Patents may feel like a natural fit if you're starting from a technical background. They are an excellent way to showcase unique problem-solving skills and establish yourself as a technical innovator.

Trade Secrets

Trade secrets protect confidential business information that provides a competitive edge. These can include:

- Recipes—the formulas for beverages or food products.
- Customer lists—detailed records of clients and prospects.

- Manufacturing processes—methods for creating materials or products.
- Software source code—valuable algorithms that companies choose not to disclose publicly.

Trade secrets are ideal for innovations better kept under wraps, where public disclosure through a patent could expose your competitive advantage.

Copyrights

Copyrights cover a wide range of creative works, such as:

- Written content—articles, whitepapers, books, and poetry
- Music and recordings—compositions and lyrics
- Visual art—paintings, digital art, and illustrations
- Software—programming instructions and code scripts

For me, copyrights were the most straightforward entry point. Writing articles, blogs, and whitepapers allowed me to share insights, build credibility, and establish my voice in the industry. They do not require registration, so they are free to obtain.

As you gain experience and generate research, consider publishing in scholarly journals or peer-reviewed conference proceedings, or publishing a book. This enables your work to be citable in research papers. If you're wondering what you have to say that's valuable, start by learning something new, connecting it to what you know, and teaching others through your unique perspective.

Trademarks

Trademarks protect the identifiers of a brand:

- Company logos—iconic symbols that define organizations
- Brand names—words that distinguish products and services
- Slogans—memorable taglines tied to a brand identity
- Packaging designs—unique shapes or styles that make products recognizable
- Mascots—characters representing a brand

Trademarks can be a valuable tool for distinguishing your work or organization and securing your position in the marketplace.

Open Source

Open source IP is when you make a contribution to a community where others are able to use your work:

- Software libraries—prebuilt tools like TensorFlow or React
- Frameworks—foundational tools such as Kubernetes for orchestration
- Open data standard implementations—formats like JavaScript Object Notation (JSON) or eXtensible Markup Language (XML) for seamless data exchange
- Hardware designs—blueprints that allow others to replicate and improve

Open source is a powerful way to learn, contribute, and collaborate while building expertise. Participating in open-source projects gives you access to vibrant communities, accelerates your skills, and creates opportunities for making meaningful contributions to shared innovation. It also allows you to work alongside experts to solve complex problems, and often opens the door to publishing copyrightable material or even generating patentable ideas. JSON and XML are also a nice lead-in to the next section—they are the actual standards that open source is based on.

Standards

Standards provide consistency, interoperability, and a shared foundation across industries. Engaging with standards development can deepen your expertise while allowing you to make a significant impact on your field.

Examples include:

- Networking protocols—foundational elements like TCP/IP
- Security frameworks—protocols such as TLS or IPsec that ensure secure communication
- File formats—standards like PDF or MP4 for universal compatibility
- Industrial standards—ISO certifications that set quality benchmarks
- Vertical specific standards—such as CAT-MIP.org

When you work on standards, you're helping to set the rules of the game for an entire industry and also meeting some incredible people. This experience often leads to new collaborations and opportunities to create additional IP, including patents and publications.

WHAT TYPE OF IP SHOULD I CREATE?

You start where you are.

- Will Allen, with over one hundred patents, has mastered system-level inventions that bridge diverse fields. His ability to connect ideas has showcased his technical expertise and established him as a trusted leader driving transformative projects at global organizations.
- Anne-Marie McReynolds started her career leveraging copyright and deep research in journalism to effect social change. She now leverages patents and mentorship to empower underrepresented groups, creating a ripple effect of innovation.
- Bill Pfeifer uses copyrights and thought leadership to elevate the work of others, crafting compelling stories and publishing widely. Bill drives actionable change and inspires cross-industry collaboration through his unique ability to connect disparate fields.
- Kathleen Moriarty exemplifies the power of standards development to shape industries. Her contributions to protocols and frameworks have positioned her as a visionary leader in security and interoperability, earning her unparalleled credibility in the field.
- Steve Todd, who uses patents and an extensive portfolio of blogs and open-source contributions, demonstrates innovation and open-source synergy. By combining these tools, Todd has influenced his organization and created a legacy of innovation that ripples across the industry.

Together, these professionals illustrate that the strategic use of IP, regardless of type, can define a career, create opportunities, and leave an indelible mark on the world.

Each of the professionals in this book has a journey showing that IP is not one-size-fits-all, and that you can create whichever type suits your needs: patents, trade secrets, copyrights, trademarks, open source, or standards. Their unique paths demonstrate how you can strategically leverage IP to amplify influence, create opportunities, and drive meaningful change.

No matter where you begin, the key is to get started. If patents feel intimidating, begin with copyrighted content. Write an article or create a white paper on something you're passionate about. If you're interested in collaboration, contribute to an open-source project or join a standards committee. These experiences will build your expertise and open doors to new opportunities, partnerships, and creations. Each step you take creates a legacy of knowledge and proof of your contributions, setting the stage for even more extraordinary achievements in the future; each IP type offers a unique entry point into the world of creation and contribution.

Patents: Protecting Inventions and Technical Innovation

A patent is a legal tool that protects an invention by giving the owner of the patent (not necessarily the inventor) exclusive rights to use, make, or sell it for a specific period—in the United States, typically twenty years. This protection ensures that no one else can copy, sell, or profit from the invention without the owners' permission. Patents also offer a way to turn ideas into financial assets through leasing or selling the ability to use the idea. To qualify for a patent, the invention must meet three key criteria: it must be new (something that hasn't been done before), useful (solving a problem or adding value), and non-obvious (not something already well-understood, or a minor change to something that already exists).

In the United States, patents are managed by the United States Patent and Trademark Office (USPTO). To obtain one, inventors must submit a detailed application describing how their invention works, why it is unique, and how it can be used. I have included the patent application we filed on the Electromagnetic Field as appendix A so you can see what one looks like. This process ensures the invention becomes part of public knowledge while giving the inventor a temporary monopoly to benefit financially. Patents are said to encourage innovation by rewarding creativity and turning groundbreaking ideas into tangible, marketable assets.

Most people submit patents through their employers who pay for the filing process. Most employment agreements include clauses claiming ownership of all inventions and patents you create during employment. If retaining ownership of your IP is essential to you, you should review your employment agreements carefully and consult with a lawyer before documenting or disclosing any new ideas.

Patents may seem complex or intimidating at first, but as Anne-Marie McReynolds puts it, they represent a skill set that can be learned and refined:

> The principle I've worked on with the patent program is you teach each person how to write the patent because there's a game to it. Some things are more patentable. There are opportunities where you can manipulate what exists today and then add embodiments on top of it. How you say thank you is you now go and help somebody else.
>
> —ANNE-MARIE McREYNOLDS

This highlights the importance of understanding the current landscape (what solutions, technologies, or ideas already exist) and building on that foundation to create something new. Adding "embodiments" means taking a concept and finding ways to improve it, apply it differently, or expand its usefulness. This approach doesn't require being a genius inventor out of the gate—it requires curiosity, creativity, and the willingness to look at existing ideas from new angles.

Generating patents isn't reserved for an elite few: it's a process of learning how to see opportunities and frame your ideas in a way that solves problems. By teaching others how to engage in this process, McReynolds fosters innovation and democratizes access to a tool that can elevate careers and amplify contributions. Her approach reminds us that creating patents is less about innate talent and more about developing a mindset and skillset that anyone can cultivate with focus and determination.

To do this, we must first understand the distinctions between a patent disclosure, a patent application, and a patent. Each plays a unique role in protecting your ideas, and knowing the differences can make or break your strategy.

THE PATENT DISCLOSURE

A patent disclosure is the starting line. It's your first formal documentation of an idea that could become a patent. Think of it as a detailed note to your employer's patent committee explaining the concept you've developed, how it works, and why it might be worth protecting. Disclosures are significant because they establish a record of when you conceived your idea and serve as a foundation for the patent application that comes next. It's not public. However, it ensures that your idea is recognized internally and, if necessary, can help prove that you were the original thinker behind it. I have included the disclosure from the initial electromagnetic idea as appendix B. (Again, no claims here that it is patentable, just an example).

THE PATENT APPLICATION

A patent application is the formal step you take on the path to securing a patent. It's like submitting your masterpiece to a jury. It is filled with technical details, claims, diagrams, and descriptions that define your invention and why it's worthy of protection. The patent office reviews your application and decides whether or not your invention is truly unique and meets all the criteria for patentability. Until it's approved, your application is in legal limbo. It is protected to some extent but not with the full force of an issued patent.

In most cases, if you are working with your employer to generate a patent, you will not be the one writing the patent application. Patent attorneys will handle that. You will be writing the disclosure.

THE PATENT

A patent is the end goal, the golden ticket. It's the official, legally binding document that says, "Yes, this invention is new; it's yours, and no one else can make, use, or sell it without the patent owners' permission." Think of it as a shield that protects your innovation in the marketplace for up to twenty years, allowing you to reap the benefits of your hard work.

This bears repeating: one key to success lies in clearly identifying a real-world problem and describing the solution in enough detail that someone skilled in the field could replicate or build it. *You do not need to build the solution to patent it.*

This realization was transformative for me. In fact, you can have an idea, write it down in great detail, and hand it off to an entirely different team for implementation. While it may seem like the people who build the technology are the inventors, that is not the case. The inventors are the ones who dream up the solution in sufficient detail so that it can be built.

This small but mighty distinction makes patents attainable for a much broader group of people, not just engineers. For years, I mistakenly believed patents were reserved for architects and those who coded software solutions. I now know that is untrue. Patents are attainable by dreamers, too.

PATENTING AT SCALE

Patents can be more than a shield for specific inventions; they can be a strategic tool to protect an entire space for future exploration. Securing patents in a particular area may leave open doors to pursue ideas and solutions down the road, creating opportunities for long-term innovation. Will Allen describes this approach as thinking beyond immediate needs to make room for what comes next.

Creating patents to protect a space can also be a competitive advantage. By filing patents in areas aligned with your business or technical expertise, you position your team to develop those ideas further without the risk of competitors encroaching on your space:

> Sometimes you're not going to build it now, but it wouldn't be bad to have a few patents of this nature.
>
> —WILL ALLEN

This mindset ensures that even if you are not ready to bring an idea to market today, you have secured the option to pursue it in the future.

While some patents may come about serendipitously—someone notices a problem and takes the initiative to solve it—patents at scale require deliberate effort. Will Allen shared how this shift in thinking helped him transition from sporadic patents to prolific innovation:

> At one point, I thought, I'm going to be more prolific. I will reach out and work with people, and then I got [to be] responsible for helping a lab generate a bunch of IP. So I made a structure.
>
> —WILL ALLEN

This intentional approach involved creating frameworks and processes that made brainstorming, refining, and filing patents a structured part of his team's work. Scaling patents also means aligning them with business goals and opportunities. As he explains,

> I try to think about what makes sense right now. You can have an idea on anything, but if it doesn't fit with the organization's strategy or needs, it might not make sense to pursue.
>
> —WILL ALLEN

This focus ensures that patents are filed for their own sake and as strategic assets supporting the company's mission.

Your ability to leverage patents at scale will depend on your corporate environment. Some organizations do not allocate substantial budgets for patenting and focus only on patenting items integrated into their products. Others invest heavily in patents as a defensive strategy. To understand your specific environment, it's essential to engage with the patent committee.

Preparing a Patent Disclosure

Once you have an idea, you will prepare a patent disclosure. You will need to gather and include specific categories of information to fully capture your invention's scope, novelty, and utility. Patent disclosures typically follow a structured format that ensures all relevant aspects of the invention are described clearly and comprehensively. Here's how to approach each section when generating a patent disclosure, along with the kinds of information you need to gather for each.

1. TITLE OF THE INVENTION

The title should be concise and informative, clearly reflecting the purpose and nature of the invention. Aim for specificity here; it helps examiners immediately understand the invention's primary function. For example, "Systematic and Programmatic Method for Creating Product Management and User Experience Research Artifacts" is direct and describes both the system and the field it applies to.

2. ABSTRACT

The abstract offers a high-level summary of the invention. Keep it under one hundred and fifty words and focus on describing the most essential parts of the invention, what it does, and why it matters. This section emphasizes the problem it solves and how your invention achieves that. In one example, we invented a method to move data proactively. The abstract is: "One example method includes data orchestration. Data sets are available to users in an online marketplace. Based on requests for data sets, other data sets may be recommended. The recommended data sets are moved or copied to recommended locations. This ensures that the data sets are available to the user more quickly if subsequently requested."

Here's how to structure it:

- Clearly define the problem your invention addresses
- Explain the core mechanism or method your invention uses to solve the problem

- Highlight any innovative technologies involved (e.g., AI, machine learning)
- Convey the importance of the invention in one to two sentences (e.g., faster production, improved accuracy, etc.)

3. BACKGROUND OF THE INVENTION

This section provides context about the field of the invention and identifies problems or inefficiencies in the current state of the art that your invention resolves. It's essential to explain what's already known in your industry and why existing methods are inadequate.

How to generate it:

- Research current industry practices and typical approaches to the problem you're solving
- Identify gaps or inefficiencies in those practices related to time, cost, accuracy, or bias (as in the provided example)
- Explain how these gaps are detrimental to the process and how they limit productivity, user experience, or development speed
- Introduce your invention as the solution, hinting at its benefits without fully explaining the mechanics

4. CURRENT PROBLEMS

Here, you'll delve deeper into the challenges that make current processes inadequate. Be specific: cite exact steps that are inefficient, prone to errors, or expensive. This section should explain why your invention is needed and how it stands apart from others currently available.

How to cover them:

- Break down the typical workflow that your invention improves
- Highlight the bottlenecks, inefficiencies, and human errors (e.g., the time-consuming nature of user journey mapping

and the prevalence of bias in decision-making, as seen in the example)

- Explain how current methods are prone to delays, inaccuracies, or inconsistencies
- Quantify the negative impact where possible (e.g., "Typically, collecting and analyzing the data requires weeks, delaying product development by X days")

This section is best supported with workflow charts.

5. INVENTION BENEFITS

This section highlights the specific advantages of your invention. Think of this as a "selling point" for patent reviewers. They need to understand why your invention is valuable and worth protecting.

Advantages should be explained like so:

- List the practical, measurable benefits (e.g., time savings, cost reductions, bias elimination)
- Tie those benefits back to the problems you identified earlier and explain how your invention resolves each issue
- Emphasize any cutting-edge technologies involved (e.g., machine learning, AI) and how they enhance your invention's capabilities
- Mention potential scalability or adaptability across industries (e.g., how the invention applies to product development in technology, healthcare, finance, etc.)

6. BRIEF DESCRIPTION OF DRAWINGS

This section provides an overview of any figures or diagrams accompanying the patent disclosure. These drawings visually represent your invention's workflow, architecture, or system components.

How to illustrate them:

- Create simple, clear diagrams or flowcharts showing your invention's key processes or structures
- Label each figure (e.g., Figure 1, Figure 2) and briefly describe what each one depicts (e.g., Figure 1 is a flowchart of the standard use case).
- Label each box in the drawing or flow chart with a detailed description of its content
- Ensure the visual elements align with the detailed descriptions in the next section

7. DETAILED DESCRIPTION

This is the heart of the patent disclosure. Here, you'll describe every component and step of your invention. Explain how the invention works, from input to output, and be as exhaustive as possible to ensure that the patent office fully understands the novelty and complexity of your idea.

How to generate it:

- Break down the invention into its main components or steps
- Describe each component's purpose and how it functions within the system
- Walk through a specific use case to demonstrate how the invention operates in practice, and include any relevant technical details, like the types of data or algorithms involved
- Connect each component or process to the problem it solves, reinforcing the importance of each part

8. OPERATIONAL FLOW OR USE CASE

This is optional but useful, as it provides a step-by-step walk-through of how your invention is used in practice. In one patent

I submitted, the operational flow shows how a product manager would input data into the system, generate a journey map, refine it, and eventually create a finalized workflow.

How to demonstrate it:

- Map out each step in the typical workflow of your invention
- Include user actions, system responses, and any iterations required
- Highlight how each step contributes to solving the problem or producing the desired output

9. CLAIMS

This section is one of the most important, as it defines the legal boundaries of your invention. Claims describe what is unique and new about your invention, specifying what aspects you want to protect. Typically, claims are written in a progressively narrowing scope, starting broad and becoming more specific.

How to describe them:

- Identify the novel elements of your invention—what sets it apart from existing solutions?
- Start with broad claims that cover the entire method or system
- Narrow down more specific claims covering individual components, processes, or features (e.g., bias detection, historian component)
- Ensure that each claim is logically connected and supported by a detailed description

If you are filing through your company, this will be enough to enter into a patent committee process.

Because I do not own the intellectual property from the patents I filed while working at organizations, and because those disclosures are considered confidential, I cannot share the details of disclosures from former employers' patents. Instead, I share a draft disclosure from the electromagnetic persona idea I mentioned earlier. Please visit appendix B for the full content.

If the disclosure is selected for filing by your organization, attorneys will assist with drafting, particularly in refining the nuances of patent claim language. The key to a strong disclosure is clear, concise writing that effectively describes what makes the invention unique and new, specifying the aspects you want to protect.

Should I Research Existing Patents When Writing My Disclosure?

The answer is that it depends—are you filing on your own or as part of an organization? If you are doing it as an employee of an organization, stop and consult with your legal team.

It might seem counterintuitive, but most organizations will advise you not to search for other patents during the invention process. Why? The short answer is liability. If you come across a similar patent and your work overlaps, you could unintentionally expose yourself and your company to accusations of willful infringement. That's a heavy charge and carries much higher penalties than if the overlap was accidental or unknowingly created. So, some legal firms will tell the inventors not to conduct patent searches, and they will deal with it on their side. Your legal team is trained to navigate the nuances of patent law. They know how to conduct prior art searches without exposing you or your organization to unnecessary risks. So, before you start doing your research, let the experts guide you. Your job is to innovate and create; theirs is to ensure your work protected in the safest, most strategic way possible. Trust them to handle the legal hurdles so you can focus on what you do best: inventing.

However, you *must* be very aware of what your competitors and other participants in the market are doing. This gives you the strength to understand the current state of the art in the field. This typically does not extend to patent searches. If you have done one, create a list of everything you looked at and submit it to the legal team with your invention. They will want this information. By looking up patents yourself, you risk absorbing concepts or language that could compromise the originality of your work.

For individual inventors, conducting a patent search can provide insights into the existing landscape, helping you ensure you're not throwing money down the drain by filing existing ideas. Approach this step with caution. If you review existing patents, you must legally disclose any known prior art to the USPTO when filing. Failing to disclose this information could lead to significant liabilities, including the invalidation of your patent if it's later challenged. While a patent search can help you strengthen your invention, it's essential to document the process carefully and consult a qualified patent attorney to ensure compliance with disclosure requirements. Understanding the risks and responsibilities of searching for patents will help you make informed decisions and avoid potential legal complications.

The USPTO offers a patent search system that allows you to browse existing patents and determine whether your invention is truly unique. The system can be accessed at https://www.uspto.gov/patents/search.

The fastest way to narrow down the millions of patents is to search the claims text for general areas of interest and use that to form a list of patents to read. To find text in the claims across the database, use the Advanced Search (at the time of writing, the direct link is https://ppubs.uspto.gov/pubwebapp/). The Advanced Search help text is inadequate, but it does the job once you get the hang of it.

Once you have generated the list of patents to examine, you must read through and determine what each patent protects. Reading the legal language of most patents is a learning experience, and I recommend extra coffee.

Filing Patents on Your Own

I have been fortunate to file some patents under my ownership. The filing process can seem overwhelming, but breaking it down into manageable steps and using resources like the USPTO makes it much more achievable. If you want to file a patent on your own, please consult with the USPTO experts during open office hours to ensure your content is in the proper format and has the correct labels. They are incredibly helpful.

Creating a patent submission requires being thorough, methodical, and precise. Each section aims to demonstrate your invention's novelty, utility, and potential impact. By gathering the correct information for each part, from abstract to claims, you will ensure that your invention is well-protected and offers a compelling case for why it deserves a patent.

I have included a full patent in appendix A so you can see the difference between a patent disclosure and an application prepared by a top patent attorney.

STEP-BY-STEP GUIDE TO FILING A PATENT ON YOUR OWN IN THE UNITED STATES

1. Determine the Type of Patent You Need

The first step is to determine the type of patent you should file. The USPTO offers three main types of patents:

- **Utility patents:** These cover new processes, machines, manufacturers, or compositions of matter. Software algorithms, mechanical inventions, and pharmaceuticals typically fall under utility patents.
- **Design patents:** These protect a manufactured item's unique appearance or design. This is ideal for someone who has created a unique product design or packaging.
- **Plant patents:** These are for anyone who invents or discovers a distinct plant variety.

Most inventors will file for a utility patent. However, it's crucial to ensure you're selecting the right type. For more information, visit the USPTO's site: https://www.uspto.gov/patents.

2. Check for Patent Eligibility

Not everything can be patented, so ensuring your invention meets the requirements is essential. To be patentable, your invention must be:

- **Novel:** It must be new and not previously known or used by others.

- **Non-obvious:** It must be a significant improvement over existing technologies or designs and not something an expert in the field could easily deduce.
- **Useful:** It must serve a purpose and be functional.

Additionally, your invention needs to be more than just an idea, it must be fully conceptualized and ready to be executed by someone who is familiar with your area of invention. In the software industry, we describe this as having enough detail that it can be implemented by someone knowledgeable in the art.

3. Prepare Your Application

Many inventors choose to work with a patent attorney at this stage. A well-drafted application can make the difference between a successful filing and a rejected one. You will have to complete the process described above to create a disclosure, format it, and add the legalese to match the requirements of the patent office. The application must include:

- **An abstract:** This is a summary (typically under one hundred and fifty words) that describes the essence of your invention.
- **A detailed description of your invention:** Be as thorough as possible. Include how it works, what makes it unique, and why it's useful.
- **Drawings:** If applicable, you must include illustrations that clearly depict your invention. You need to number each section of your drawing and include complete written details related to the drawing section. If you can, create your illustrations and diagrams in black and white. There is an upcharge for any color drawings.

- **Claims:** These define the boundaries of what your patent will protect. Be specific, as these claims will determine the legal scope of your patent.

The electronic application requires that these sections be uploaded separately.

4. File Your Application

Once your application is ready, you can submit it to the USPTO. The easiest and most efficient way to file is through the USPTO's Electronic Filing System (EFS-Web) at https://www.uspto.gov/patents/apply.

You'll need to create an account if you don't already have one. Once logged in, you can upload your application documents, pay the filing fee, and officially submit your patent application. The costs vary depending on the type of patent, filing category (individual, small entity, or large company), and the complexity of the application.

Filing fees for utility patents are typically under $1,000 USD, but they can increase if your application requires multiple claims or if you're requesting an expedited review. The small and micro-organization filing options (solo entrepreneur) are much less expensive. You can check the current fee schedule here: https://www.uspto.gov/learning-and-resources/fees-and-payment.

5. Respond to USPTO Communications

After submission, a patent examiner will review your application. During this process, the examiner may issue an Office

Action, which outlines objections or issues with your application. You typically receive a letter notifying you of an electronic notification in your inbox. My first several personal filings were rejected. Do not panic or take it personally. Simply respond and amend your application if necessary.

Attending the USPTO office hours or working with a patent attorney at this stage can be invaluable. They can help you draft a response that addresses the examiner's concerns and keeps your application moving forward.

If your application is approved, congratulations! You'll receive an official Notice of Allowance and will need to pay an additional issuance fee before your patent is granted. Once paid, your patent will be officially registered, and you'll receive a certificate confirming your patent rights.

The first question most people ask is how long this takes. If you pay an expedition fee and are on a fast track where the field of invention is prioritized, your patent may be reviewed and publicly visible in as little as six months. In my own experience, a wait period of one and a half to two years is more typical.

It is important to note that most patents are made public. When you invent something and file a patent, the full content of that patent is generally available for anyone to read. That is why trade secrets are another noteworthy type of IP.

What Are the Odds of Getting a Patent Granted?

Not great, but better than zero. Erik Heels, a patent lawyer at Clocktower Law (www.clocktowerlaw.com), offers insightful perspective on inventors' challenges when pursuing a patent. According to Heels, the odds of obtaining a patent are roughly 50–50, and the system often feels stacked against inventors. He explains that complex requirements like "nonobviousness" and additional hurdles such as "subject matter eligibility" frequently lead to confusion and frustration. Additionally, patent examiners are incentivized to "dispose of" applications, often resulting in delays and rejections intended to discourage applicants.

However, Heels emphasizes that inventors can improve their odds by taking proactive steps. He recommends conducting thorough patent searches with proper disclosure and submitting strong, well-prepared applications to increase the likelihood of success. With these measures, Heels suggests that inventors can move their odds closer to 55–45, a meaningful improvement that could make the difference between obtaining a patent or walking away empty-handed.

This success rate aligns with my own experiences. I found a slightly higher rate of granted patents for entirely new areas of invention, such as those involving advanced technologies like terahertz (THz) networks. In contrast, fields with many existing inventions, such as backup and data protection, had a lower success rate. This highlights the importance of understanding the competitive landscape and preparing thoroughly to maximize the chances of success.

Provisional Filing

Filing a provisional is a tactical tool that allows you to stake your invention claim early without committing to the full process upfront. By filing a provisional application, you establish an official filing date for your invention while giving yourself up to twelve months to refine the details before filing a full patent. This is valuable in a number of situations: if you're iterating on a concept, gathering funding, needing to disclose your idea, waiting on resources to free up, or even still in the midst of determining commercial viability. It is a relatively inexpensive way to save your place in line if you do choose to pursue the patent.

A common misconception is that a provisional patent offers full protection. It doesn't. Provisional applications never become patents on their own. They are context-aware placeholders. You must convert them into patent applications within twelve months, or you lose the priority date.

Additionally, your provisional must contain enough detail to fully describe your invention. If you file an overly vague provisional and later try to claim an invention with additional details that weren't originally included, those new details won't receive the original filing date, potentially invalidating them. The disclosure example in appendix B is one example of the amount of detail which could be included in a provisional.

If you're certain about moving forward, a direct patent filing might be the better path.

TRADE SECRETS: PROTECTING CONFIDENTIAL BUSINESS INFORMATION

Trade secrets protect confidential business information from being disclosed or used without authorization. Trade secrets can include formulas, practices, processes, designs, instruments, or a compilation of information that provides a business with a competitive edge. A famous example of a trade secret is the formula for Coke, which has been kept secret for over a century. Unlike patents or copyrights, trade secrets are not registered with the government, and their protection relies on maintaining confidentiality.

In my work, trade secrets have been crucial for protecting proprietary algorithms and technical processes, especially in AI and machine learning. For example, while some algorithms we developed could be patented, other aspects of the business, such as our approach to training models or specific machine learning optimizations, were better protected as trade secrets. Maintaining confidentiality in these areas ensured competitors could not easily replicate our methods.

The key to generating and maintaining trade secrets is safeguarding critical information and implementing security measures to prevent leaks. This can involve using nondisclosure agreements (NDAs), limiting access to sensitive information, and ensuring that only trusted employees know the trade secret. It is useful to consult with a legal expert on any formalities that are required to protect trade secrets.

Trade secrets are exceptional for internal validation and internal career growth. However, for obvious reasons (you can't talk about them), they are poor tools for getting a job at an external organization.

COPYRIGHTS: PROTECTING LITERARY, ARTISTIC, AND SOFTWARE CREATIONS

Copyright protects original works of authorship such as books, software, research, music, video, and art once they are fixed in a tangible form (written, recorded, or coded). The owner holds exclusive rights to reproduce, share, perform, display, and create derivative works.

Creating copyrighted material is straightforward: write an article, record music, or publish code. As long as it's original and tangible, it's protected.

While you do not have to register copyrighted material, you may do so to provide a public record of your ownership, defend your work against copyright infringement, and transfer your rights if desired.

If you work for a corporation, your employment agreement may grant them ownership of the material you generate. Also, when you post or share your IP online or via a publisher, the terms of service often give the platform a license to use, distribute, or display your content. This doesn't mean you lose your copyright, but it does grant the platform certain rights to use your content as long as it remains on their site. Consider looking at the terms of service before publishing.

Many of us will create multiple forms of copyright material using the written word, images (infographics, diagrams), video or audio content (podcasts/webinars), and code. For people building their career, thought leadership is particularly effective for creating meaningful content for copyright.

Building Your Reputation with Thought Leadership Copyrights

Thought leadership is a strategic way to establish yourself or your organization as a trusted expert. It's about sharing unique insights, perspectives, and real solutions that others haven't thought of or dared to express. True thought leaders speak to real issues, offer valuable solutions, and connect ideas across disciplines. You'll find their influence growing through articles, speaking engagements, social media, interviews, and white papers, reaching people at every level and drawing in those who care about these ideas, too. If you are unfamiliar with what thought leaders do, consider watching Ted Talks to find a few who resonate with you. Seth Godin and Sheryl Sandberg are two people who do this exceptionally well.

Do not confuse the LinkedIn badge or social media concept of "influencer" with thought leadership. Bill Pfeifer, a seasoned host of multiple technology thought leadership podcasts, offers a transformative perspective on the essence of authentic leadership in this space. He explains:

> Thought leadership isn't about saying who I am; it's about asking how I can guide people to move in the direction of impactful change.
>
> —BILL PFEIFER

This insight frames the purpose of thought leadership: it is not self-proclaimed but recognized through actions that drive forward progress. This redefinition positions thought leadership not as a title but as an ongoing act of creating influence through meaningful contributions and inspiring change.

This kind of work is not always easy; when you step forward with new ideas or challenge existing norms, resistance often follows. Thought leadership asks us to see the world differently, and that can make people uncomfortable. Some resistance comes from genuine concerns about confidentiality or alignment with company strategy. Other times, it's personal—colleagues might feel left out, or worry they're being overshadowed.

Understanding where that resistance comes from is essential. It helps you respond with empathy, rather than defensiveness, and find the right path forward.

Steve Todd has lived this. He shares what happened when he first started blogging about the industry:

> I was unpopular. Some colleagues said, 'You shouldn't be doing that'. That's bragging. Or who do you think you are to say that stuff? But the big, the most unpopular thing that happened was

executives began telling me to stop and how dare I share my opinions on corporate strategy or the industry without running it through the marketing department.

—STEVE TODD

What Todd experienced is all too common: his peers misunderstood his intentions, and his leaders saw him stepping outside traditional communication channels. But over time, his voice stood out. He wasn't trying to disrupt for the sake of it. He was trying to help. And eventually, that became clear.

Despite the resistance, Todd's decision to share his insights elevated his visibility, positioned him as a thought leader, and ultimately differentiated him within his company.

Whether addressing peers' concerns or aligning with company policies, thought leadership demands resilience and the ability to push forward while fostering trust and collaboration. Todd's journey reminds us that effective thought leadership is not about defiance but about creating value, even when facing challenges.

Unlike traditional marketing, which often promotes products or services, thought leadership focuses on sharing perspectives, building trust, and fostering connections by offering sound, forward-thinking ideas. Creating thought leadership content for enterprises often leads to greater brand loyalty and influence. For you, it can mean more opportunity and leverage to do the type of work you want to do and justify promotions.

When I began working with machine learning in 2004, I published detailed articles on building algorithms using machine learning platforms. These were highly technical pieces, often focused on combining image processing techniques for specific outcomes, and were featured in publications like the *Journal of Scientific Computing*. That visibility led to speaking opportunities at research conferences and raised my profile within the company.

One unexpected opportunity was a talk at a Drosophila research conference. I wasn't an expert in fruit flies or genetics, but I was an expert in APIs and automation. Our project applied ML algorithms to automate image analysis of fruit fly specimens, including counting, mutation detection, and other tasks that were traditionally manual and error-prone. Automating this process saved researchers time and improved consistency.

To ensure my presentation resonated with the audience, I partnered with one of the Drosophila researchers from Sandia National Laboratories to understand their challenges and objectives. This collaboration allowed me to frame the technical aspects of the project in a way that connected with their work and addressed their needs. By bridging my technical expertise with their domain knowledge, we created a shared narrative that advanced understanding and encouraged further collaboration. It was a powerful reminder that thought leadership isn't about knowing everything; it's about leveraging your expertise to make meaningful contributions and helping others move forward together.

Today, I focus on forward-looking ideas and strategic horizons. I conduct formal and informal research and speak with hundreds of customers and industry leaders annually to gather data. I then analyze this research to consider the implications of emerging trends. I now speak at conferences and give press interviews on AI, sharing my predictions on how the market may evolve over the next three to five years.

As with my overall professional journey, my journey through thought leadership has unfolded in stages. And, just as with my patent journey, it was not until I spoke with one of my mentors that I realized there were frameworks for thought leadership.

My frequent collaborator and mentor, Debra Slapak, who coauthored *Compassion-Driven Innovation*, generated a table (table 3.1) that approximates the stages of thought leadership and provides examples of credibility-building strategies.

This is one way to consider thought leadership as a framework. There does seem to be a natural alignment on the types of articles you can create based on your depth of experience, but in theory, anyone can produce any kind of article. Whether or not

TABLE 3.1 STAGES OF THOUGHT LEADERSHIP

Thought leadership level	Credibility-building strategies
Practical thought leader	• Publish regularly online • Share practical insights • Source insights from conversations with peers, customers, and other thought leaders
Progressive thought leader	• Collaborate with other experts • Present at conferences • Use research data and anecdotes to prove points • Publish targeted, in-depth content
Transformational thought leader	• Conduct original research • Publish on high-impact platforms • Lead workshops about establishing oneself as a thought leader or about specific thought leadership subject matter • Share potentially game-changing perspectives via extended works such as books
Visionary thought leader	• Promote future-oriented ideas with strategic horizons • Engage in media appearances and high-profile speaking opportunities • Mentor emerging leaders

it will resonate, however, is an interesting and important consideration. For example, I doubt anybody would consider a visionary article from me on veterinarian practices remotely credible (and rightly so; I have no experience in the field).

> Developing expertise in thought leadership is much like progressing in any career path. It requires building knowledge and honing communication skills to reach your goals. You need to decide which subjects to focus on, dedicate time to becoming an expert in those areas, and learn how to share compelling stories with your chosen audience. What are your goals relative to the kind of thought leader you want to be?
>
> —DEBRA SLAPAK

There's no rule that says everyone must aspire to be a "visionary thought leader"; most people aren't comfortable in that category. You can be whatever kind of thought leader you want to be:

- You can be wildly successful as a practical thought leader, publishing effective "how to" articles.
- You can create an entire career centered around transformational thought leadership, conducting research, speaking, and going on podcasts without having to project the future.

There is a whole career path for this if it suits your personality. The possibilities are endless. But, as someone who went the first few decades without strategic direction, take it from me and save yourself some time and effort. Consider what your larger goals are and see if one of those levels resonates with you. By intentionally pursuing a path, you can be more successful with less work and less pressure.

Kathleen Moriarty is an exceptional example of a visionary thought leader. She works tirelessly to elevate the entire industry through publications and speaking engagements. In her book, *Transforming Information Security: Optimizing Five Concurrent Trends to Reduce Resource Drain*, she openly shares architectural patterns designed for scalability, with the intention that others will build upon them to drive meaningful improvements. She has also published a white paper and coordinated it with an RSA365 webinar, further planting the seeds for building security at scale.

HOW TO WRITE A THOUGHT LEADERSHIP ARTICLE: A STEP-BY-STEP PROCESS

If you decide that thought leadership is worth pursuing, consider writing an article or two. To make an impact, consider writing an article built on engaging ideas supported by research, customer stories, or expert insights. The goal is to package these ideas in a way that informs and leaves a lasting impression on your readers.

For people who aren't writers, you can use the process below to craft a thought leadership video, conference talk, or even podcast. The process starts with identifying a topic that aligns with your expertise and addresses a pressing need or question in your industry.

Here's a step-by-step process to guide you through crafting an article for a high-credibility industry publication.

1. Choose a Relevant, Timely Topic

When identifying a topic to write or speak about, relevance and timing are everything. Start with what your audience cares about now. For instance, are there emerging trends or technological innovations that are creating new opportunities or challenges? Are there changes in industry standards, customer needs, or regulatory environments? Your goal should be to reveal insights that help your audience navigate these shifts. This means anticipating what they need to know and answering questions they may not have thought to ask yet.

Bill Pfeifer emphasized the power of asking meaningful questions and connecting ideas across disciplines. He explained:

> You have to have some area of expertise and some ability to connect that to something that people care about. It's less about what you know and more about how you think about stuff, how you ideate, and how creative you are in making connections between different disciplines, ideas, and people.
>
> —BILL PFEIFER

This ability to see patterns and articulate their implications is essential for authentic thought leadership that makes an impact.

To discover timely topics, you can:

- Engage with customers to understand their most pressing challenges
- Attend conferences, webinars, and forums to track industry conversations
- Read industry reports and white papers to identify underdiscussed themes
- Examine your own work and identify patterns or insights that could benefit others

To ensure your topic reflects your unique perspective. Pfeifer elaborated:

> Being a generalist helps you connect ideas across disciplines. We find something interesting and connect it back to the broader conversation in a way others haven't thought of yet. By focusing on connections and building bridges, your thought leadership becomes not only relevant but also essential.
>
> —BILL PFEIFER

Whether you're writing an article, presenting at a conference, or participating in a podcast, the process begins with finding the right topic. Use these strategies and examples to ensure your voice resonates, stands out, and provides tangible value to your audience.

2. Understand Your Target Audience and Publication Platform

Consider the audience that would most benefit from your idea and perspectives. Who do you want to inform? What are the platforms they turn to for expertise? Platforms work to differentiate from other platforms to attract readers, so the tone, style, and depth of your article should align with their expectations. For example, are you writing for C-suite executives who want high-level insights and strategic advice? Or is your audience primarily technical experts who prefer detailed, data-driven content?

Browse recent posts or articles on the platforms of interest to get a sense of the kind of content they publish. What's the balance between thought leadership and actionable advice? Are they more formal or conversational in tone? Understanding the publication's audience and publication criteria helps you create an article that resonates with the right people and increases your chances of getting published.

At this stage, you should contact your marketing organization. They may have certain platforms with paid media opportunities to post your article and promote it via their social channels. They may have suggestions to help you focus your content so that it will lead to their content and pull audiences into your funnel.

3. Provide Value and Insight

Readers don't want articles that restate the obvious; they're looking for insights they can't get anywhere else. Draw on your experience to provide unique perspectives, predictions for the future, or in-depth analysis of the problem you're addressing.

Incorporate relevant data and research to support your points: include statistics, charts, or findings from reputable studies to enhance your credibility and give your article substance. Remember, don't overwhelm your reader with too much technical jargon. Keep the information accessible, especially for publications that cater to a broader audience.

4. Develop a Clear Outline

Now, it's time to map out your article. Consider the unique experiences you have had. How can you relate them to the topic at hand? Begin with a clear structure to guide your writing.

A typical outline for an industry article looks like this:

- **Introduction:** Grab the reader's attention right away. Introduce the problem, trend, or topic you're addressing and why it matters now. This is your hook.
- **Body:** Break down the issue into digestible sections, each addressing a specific point or subtopic. A typical story arc:
    - Begins with an anecdote or statistic that introduces opportunities for change from the status quo. What are the issues that demand change, and why? What are the opportunities that change presents?

  - What are the obstacles to this change, how can they be removed, and who should take action?
  - What happens if organizations don't lead or participate in removing these obstacles?
  - What are the steps organizations can take now to move forward?
  - Back up your insights with data, case studies, or real-world examples. Include actionable takeaways that your readers can apply to their own work.
- **Conclusion:** Wrap up your article with a strong call to action or closing thought. Summarize the key points and leave the reader with something to think about, whether it's a new perspective, an innovative solution, or a direction (including links) for future exploration.

If you're not experienced at telling stories or want to polish your techniques, consider *Storyteller Tactics*® by Steve Rawling. It's a card deck of more than 50 different fun and unique storytelling techniques for compiling ideas and information so that people will want to read, watch, or otherwise engage with your ideas. Many excellent storytelling books and courses are also available, such as *TED Talks Storytelling* by Akash Karia. Online platforms such as LinkedIn Learning and Coursera also offer classes.

Planning your article in advance helps you stay organized and ensures that your ideas flow logically and build on each other.

5. Write with Clarity and Precision

Before you start writing, review the submission guidelines for your target publication(s). Ensure your article fits within their word count, format, and topic preferences.

Write your article so it is clear and easy to follow, with concise but varied sentences and a logical flow from one point to the next. Avoid the temptation to use overly complex language or industry jargon. Your goal is to communicate your ideas as clearly and effectively as possible.

That said, don't be afraid to inject a little personality or creativity into your writing. A well-placed anecdote, an interesting metaphor, or a touch of humor can make your article more engaging and memorable.

6. Edit, Edit, Edit

Editing is just as important as writing. Once you've finished your draft, step away for a day or two, then return to it with fresh eyes. Look for areas where you can tighten up your writing, eliminate redundancies, cut unnecessary words, and clarify any complex ideas. Read your draft aloud to catch awkward phrasing or sentences that don't flow smoothly. Use Grammarly™ or similar software to check your work for errors and get stylistic recommendations.

Ask someone else to review your article. A second pair of eyes will catch mistakes you missed and provide valuable feedback on the overall structure and content of your article.

7. Submit with Confidence

If you're not working through your marketing organization for publication, tailor your pitch email to your target publication, explaining why your article is relevant and timely for their audience.

Once you've submitted your article, be patient and follow up politely if you haven't heard back within their typical response time. Whether accepted or not, writing and submitting an article strengthens your skills as a thought leader, and each experience helps you grow.

I find it satisfying when one of my thought leadership articles gets an "earned media" placement. This occurs when editors of respected platforms choose to publish your article because they see it as compelling, relevant, and valuable without requiring you or your employer to pay for the placement.

An earned media placement validates the importance of your ideas and your place as an authority in your field. Gaining this level of recognition requires thoughtfulness in crafting your article to ensure it reflects your expertise and connects deeply with the audience's needs. By following a process, you can create content that stands out and builds your reputation as a trusted voice in your industry.

If you are not published by others, you can always release your articles yourself. Consider directly posting to Medium, Substack, LinkedIn, or another platform where your target audience will encounter the work.

While this section is aimed at the writing process, as that is my preferred artifact type, consider it an outline for any medium type. By following this process, you can write and submit an industry article that reflects your expertise and resonates with your target audience. Stay true to your voice, provide value, and always aim to contribute something meaningful to the ongoing conversation in your field.

Building Your Reputation with Code Copyrights

While thought leadership and presentation often take the spotlight in discussions about intellectual property, building your reputation with code and other portfolio copyrights is an equally powerful way to establish expertise and influence. Code is tangible evidence of your skills, insights, and problem-solving ability.

It can showcase your contributions and can be shared broadly, opening doors to new opportunities.

Publishing code is one of the most direct ways to demonstrate technical expertise. Whether it's contributing to projects on platforms like GitHub or creating proprietary tools within your organization, sharing well-documented, functional code signals your ability to solve problems effectively.

Step-by-Step Guide to Generating and Filing for Copyright in the United States

Copyright protection automatically applies to original works of authorship the moment they are fixed in a tangible form. For most creators, this built-in protection is sufficient. However, if your work is highly original, influential, or groundbreaking, you may choose to file for formal copyright registration. This step strengthens your legal rights and allows you to pursue statutory damages and attorney fees in the event of infringement.

I copyrighted this book, just as I did with my previous two books. Copyrighting my work ensures that it is protected while providing a foundation for me to share insights and contribute to thought leadership without worrying about unauthorized use. It also ensures that your work can be cited. This process is straightforward, but it's essential to understand the steps involved.

1. Create an Original Work

The first step to obtaining a copyright is simple: you must create something original. Copyright protection applies to "original works of authorship" that are fixed in a tangible medium. This means your work needs to be more than just an idea; it must be written down, recorded, or otherwise documented in a way that is concrete and demonstrable.

Examples of works that can be copyrighted include:

- Literary works (e.g., novels, poems, blog posts)
- Scholarly and reference works (e.g., analyses, white papers, textbooks, research databases)
- Visual art (e.g., illustrations, photography, graphic designs)
- Music compositions and sound recordings
- Software code
- Architectural designs

Once your original work is complete and "fixed," it's automatically protected by copyright law. However, filing with the US Copyright Office (USCO) or local equivalent gives you added legal protection and a public record of your ownership.

2. **Determine Eligibility**

Before you file, you must ensure your work is eligible for copyright protection. According to the USCO, the work must:

- Be an original creation
- Be fixed in a tangible form of expression
- Contain a minimum level of creativity (basic factual information, short phrases, or titles aren't eligible)

For example, a novel you've written, or a photograph you've taken is eligible, though a two-word slogan might not be. That is likelier to be a trademark.

3. Prepare Your Materials

To file for copyright, you'll need the following:

- A digital or physical copy of the work you want to register
- Basic information about the work, such as the title, author's name, and creation date
- A small filing fee

Make sure your work is ready in its final form because the version you submit is the one protected by copyright. Revisions made after filing would require separate registration.

4. Submit an Application

You can file your copyright application online through USCO's electronic system, eCO, or by mail. The online route is faster, more cost-effective, and easier to track.

- **Online:** Visit the eCO website https://eco.copyright.gov/. Log in or create an account. Follow the steps to complete your application, providing the necessary details about your work and uploading a copy of it.
- **By mail:** If you prefer, you can download the appropriate forms from the USCO website https://www.copyright.gov/forms/, fill them out, and send them along with the required fee and a copy of your work.

Online applications tend to be processed faster, often within three to four months. Mail submissions can take up to nine months, so consider that timeline if you work under a deadline.

You will select the type of work (in my case, typically written), confirm ownership of the work, and enter your contact information.

There is a decision you will need to make on privacy. If you choose to have yourself as the primary contact, your information may be publicly available. Some people set up a company to manage their copyrights and use a post office box or other address to protect their information.

5. Pay the Filing Fee

The filing fee depends on the method of submission and the type of work. For most single works, the fee for an online application is $65. You'll pay the fee during the application process or by check if filing by mail.

6. Submit Your Work

Once you've completed the application and paid the fee, you'll need to upload or mail a copy of your work. For digital content (e.g., manuscripts, music files, or artwork), you can usually upload a file directly through the eCO system. If you're submitting physical work, such as a painting or sculpture, you'll send a physical copy or photograph of the work.

The submission process for physical items is explained in detail on the USCO website https://www.copyright.gov/. They also provide instructions on the required format for digital submissions.

7. Receive Your Certificate of Registration

After your application is reviewed and approved, you'll receive a Certificate of Registration (figure 3.2). This certificate is an official document verifying your copyright claim. Hold onto it. It's your legal proof of ownership, and you will need it should you have to take action against copyright infringement.

After obtaining a copyright, placing a © notice with the date and name of its owner on the work establishes your ownership and serves as notice to others that your work is protected.

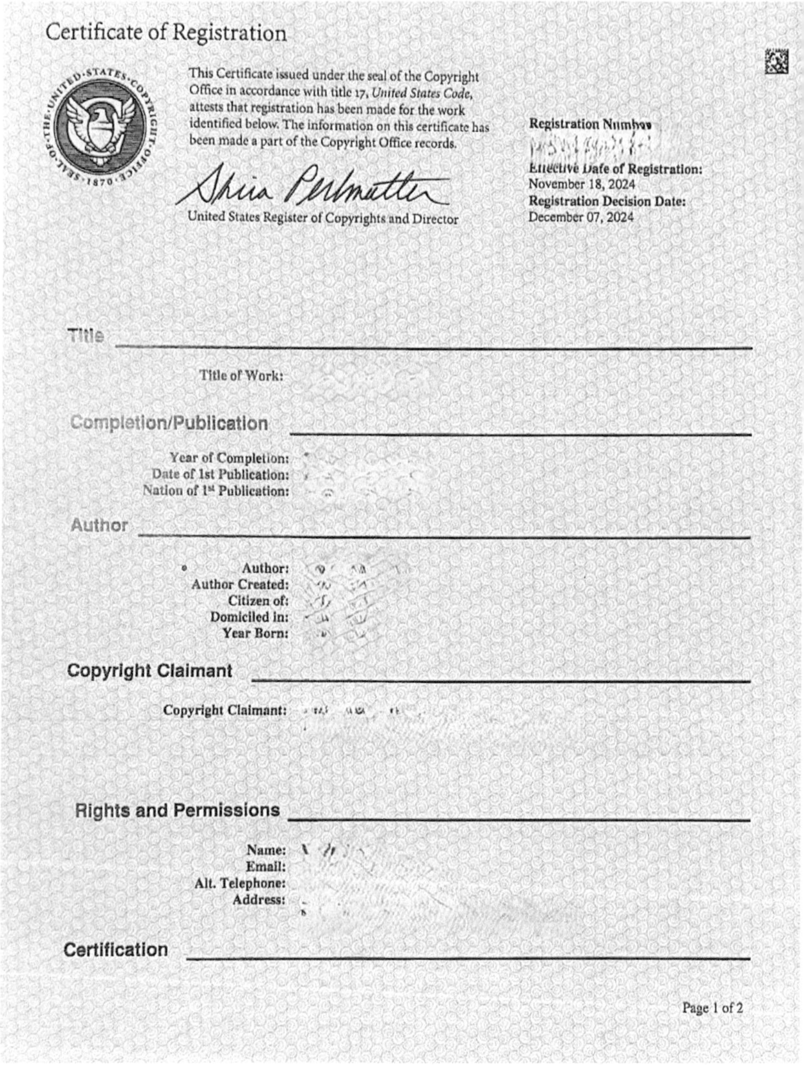

Certificate of Registration

This Certificate issued under the seal of the Copyright Office in accordance with title 17, *United States Code*, attests that registration has been made for the work identified below. The information on this certificate has been made a part of the Copyright Office records.

United States Register of Copyrights and Director

Registration Number [illegible]

Effective Date of Registration:
November 18, 2024

Registration Decision Date:
December 07, 2024

Title

Title of Work: [illegible]

Completion/Publication

Year of Completion: [illegible]
Date of 1st Publication: [illegible]
Nation of 1st Publication: [illegible]

Author

- Author: [illegible]
  Author Created: [illegible]
  Citizen of: [illegible]
  Domiciled in: [illegible]
  Year Born: [illegible]

Copyright Claimant

Copyright Claimant: [illegible]

Rights and Permissions

Name: [illegible]
Email: [illegible]
Alt. Telephone: [illegible]
Address: [illegible]

Certification

Page 1 of 2

FIGURE 3.2 Certificate of Registration for USCO.
(Photo by Nicole Reineke.)

Copyright is one of the most straightforward ways to protect your creative work, and the process of filing is easier than you might think. By following these steps and using the USCO's resources, you can ensure your original works are protected, giving you peace of mind as you continue to create.

TRADEMARKS: PROTECTING BRANDS, SYMBOLS, AND COMMERCE

A trademark is a symbol, word, phrase, design, or combination of these elements that distinguishes the goods or services of one company from those of others. Once registered, a trademark gives the owner exclusive rights to use the mark in commerce and prevents others from using a similar mark that could cause confusion among consumers.

In my experience, trademarks are used to build and protect brand identity. Although much of my work has focused on technical innovations, I have been involved in projects that required branding new products or technologies. In these cases, we developed trademarks for the names and symbols associated with our brand. This step ensured that our brand was protected and recognizable in the competitive tech marketplace.

Generating a trademark requires creating a unique name, logo, or design that sets a product apart. After creating the mark, it must be registered with a government office (such as the USPTO) to be granted formal protection. Trademark holders must also maintain the mark's usage in commerce and take action to defend it if others attempt to infringe on their rights.

Step-by-Step Guide to Filing a Trademark in the United States

1. Determine What You Want to Trademark

Before you can file a trademark, you need to decide what exactly you're protecting. A trademark can be anything that identifies and distinguishes your goods or services from those of others. This could be:

- A word or phrase (e.g., Magic Quadrant™ by Gartner®)
- A logo (e.g., an apple with a bite taken out, created by Apple®)
- A slogan (e.g., Think Different™ by Apple)
- A product packaging design, or even a sound or color in some cases.

Trademarks only protect elements used in commerce. If you haven't used your mark yet, you can file based on an "intent to use." However, you will need to show actual use before the trademark is registered. Also, a trademark doesn't mean you "own" a design, word, or phrase. It means you have the right to use that item in the context of your industry. For example, Apple holds the trademark for its name used in technology like smartphones and TV, but it can't stop someone from naming their child "Apple" or selling the fruit. Trademarks protect the association of a word, phrase, or design within your goods or services.

Key guidelines:

- ™ is used for an unregistered trademark to indicate that you are claiming rights to the brand.
- ® is used for a registered trademark to show that it is officially recognized and protected by law.

- For phrases, slogans, or logos, always ensure that the appropriate symbol is used—either ™ or ®, depending on the registration status.

2. Conduct a Trademark Search

You'll need to ensure that no one else has already registered a similar trademark that could cause confusion with yours. The USPTO provides a free search system called TESS (Trademark Electronic Search System), where you can search existing trademarks to ensure your proposed mark is available.

Visit https://www.uspto.gov/trademarks/search to access TESS and search for trademarks that might conflict with yours. Search for exact matches and for marks that are phonetically similar or use similar designs.

Skipping this step could result in wasted time and money if your application is rejected because a similar trademark already exists.

3. Choose Your Filing Basis

In the United States, you can file for a trademark on one of two bases:

- **"Use in Commerce":** You are already using the trademark in the sale of goods or services.
- **"Intent to Use":** You haven't started using the mark yet, but plan to in the near future.

Applicants in the early stages of building their brand will file under the "Intent to Use" basis, allowing them time to start using the trademark before fully registering it. If you file under "Intent to Use," you must submit additional proof once the trademark is actively used in commerce.

4. **Prepare Your Application**

Next, you'll prepare your trademark application. You can do this online through the USPTO's Trademark Electronic Application System (TEAS) at https://www.uspto.gov/trademarks/apply. The application will ask for details about your trademark, including:

- The specific goods or services your trademark will apply to (e.g., software, apparel, marketing services)
- Your filing basis (either "Use in Commerce" or "Intent to Use")
- A drawing or image of your mark, if applicable (e.g., a logo)
- A description of how your trademark will be used in commerce

Take your time with this step to ensure everything is clear and accurate. A clear description of the goods or services your trademark will apply to is key to successful and meaningful registration. If you're unsure about any of the details, consulting with a trademark attorney can save you time and headaches later.

5. **Submit the Application and Pay the Filing Fee**

Once your application is complete, you'll submit it through the TEAS system and pay the filing fee. The fee for filing a trademark depends on how many categories of goods or services you're registering the mark for. As of 2026, filing fees typically range from $250 to $350 per class of goods/services.

Choose the correct form based on your specific needs:

- **TEAS Plus:** $250 per class, which requires stricter adherence to USPTO's requirements
- **TEAS Standard:** $350 per class, offering more flexibility in your application

For a complete list of fees and application types, visit: https://www.uspto.gov/trademarks/trademark-fee-information.

6. Monitor Your Application

After you file, your application will be assigned to a USPTO examining attorney. The attorney will review your application to ensure it meets all legal requirements and doesn't conflict with any existing trademarks. This process typically takes anywhere from eight to twelve months, though it can be longer depending on the complexity of the application.

You may receive an Office Action from the USPTO if the attorney finds any issues or conflicts with your application. If this happens, you'll need to respond within six months, addressing the concerns or amending your application.

7. Receive Your Trademark Registration

Once your application is approved, you'll receive a Notice of Publication, meaning your trademark will be published in the Official Gazette to allow anyone to challenge it. If no opposition is filed, your trademark will be registered, and you'll receive a certificate of registration from the USPTO.

If you filed under "Intent to Use," you must submit a Statement of Use to prove your mark is now in commerce before receiving the official registration.

Filing a trademark is an essential step in protecting your brand identity, ensuring that your logo, name, or slogan is legally yours to use. By following this step-by-step guide and utilizing the USPTO's resources, you can navigate the trademark process with confidence and safeguard your brand for years to come. For more information and to begin the filing process, visit https://www.uspto.gov.

OPEN SOURCE

Open source is more than just freely available code. It is a dynamic ecosystem fueled by collaboration, innovation, and shared expertise. Projects like Kubernetes, Linux, and TensorFlow began as open-source initiatives and have since become indispensable components of the technology stacks used by the world's largest organizations. By contributing to open-source projects, individuals not only help advance critical technologies, but also create a visible record of their work, establishing credibility in their field and building their professional reputation.

At its core, open source thrives on the principle of shared knowledge. When you participate in open-source projects, you join a global network of developers, researchers, and innovators working together to solve complex problems. This collaborative model significantly benefits individuals, companies, and industries alike.

One of the most remarkable aspects of open source is its ability to accelerate innovation. Unlike proprietary initiatives, which are often limited to internal resources, open-source projects leverage the collective intelligence of a community. This inclusivity fosters creativity and allows solutions to develop quickly. Open source also reduces startup costs for organizations, enabling them to avoid the expense of building solutions from scratch. By utilizing and contributing to open-source software, companies can focus their resources on driving additional value.

For individuals, engaging with open source is an unparalleled opportunity to build expertise. These projects often involve cutting-edge technologies, allowing participants to deepen their technical skills and learn from experienced community members. Perhaps one of the most significant advantages is the visibility open source provides. Contributions are publicly accessible, allowing you to create a portfolio demonstrating your expertise to peers, potential employers, and collaborators.

Open-source contributions can take many forms:

- Code Contributions: Writing new code, fixing bugs, or improving performance
- Design Work: Creating icons, UI/UX designs or other visual assets
- Documentation and Writing: Improving project documentation, creating tutorials, or writing blogs about your experiences
- Community Engagement: Answering questions, moderating forums, or organizing meetups
- Marketing and Social Media: Promoting projects, creating educational content, or building awareness

Every one of these contributions represents a piece of intellectual property. While you may not "own" the project, your contributions are tied to your name and expertise.

Despite its benefits, open source is not without challenges. Steve Todd's experience in leading the Alvarium project from a private implementation to an open-source project underscores the obstacles many face when proposing open-source initiatives in traditional organizations. Concerns about intellectual property, security, and the potential risks of sharing resulting in revenue lost are common. As Todd explains, advocating for open source can be challenging but immensely rewarding. He shares:

> Open source can be risky for a company, and it took significant persuasion on my part to say, 'Listen, I'm going to stick with this and follow it through, and I'll make sure that nothing bad

> happens.' In the end, the answer was yes. It was one of the hardest things I've done but also one of the things I'm most proud of.
>
> —STEVE TODD

Technology initiatives, such as open source, can sometimes face resistance from leadership. To address these challenges, it is essential to align your vision with the organization's strategic priorities. Clearly articulate how open source contributes to key goals like fostering innovation, attracting top talent, or entering new markets. Proactively address potential risks by presenting well-thought-out mitigation strategies and highlighting the safeguards you will put in place to protect the organization's interests. This approach demonstrates foresight and reassures leadership that your initiative is aligned with their objectives and carefully planned for success.

Getting Started with Open Source: A Step-by-Step Guide

Contributing to open source can seem intimidating at first, but the key is to start small and focus on projects that align with your interests and goals. Open source is a powerful way to showcase your expertise, collaborate with others, and make meaningful impact. Here's how to begin:

1. Choose a Project That Aligns with Your Interests

The best way to stay motivated is by contributing to projects that excite you or align with your long-term goals. Start by identifying your areas of interest:

- **Cloud Computing:** Explore projects like Kubernetes, Docker, or Terraform.

- **Artificial Intelligence:** Dive into TensorFlow, PyTorch, or Hugging Face.
- **Graphic Design:** Look for projects needing help with branding, UI/UX, or visual elements.

When you work on something you're passionate about, your enthusiasm will show in your contributions, and you'll naturally want to learn and grow within the community.

2. Assess Project Activity

Not all open-source projects are created equal. To ensure your efforts have a real impact, focus on projects with active and engaged communities. Look for indicators such as:

- Regularly accepted and merged pull requests
- Active discussions and resolutions in the issues section
- Contributors engaging on platforms like Discord, Slack, or mailing lists

Projects with healthy activity levels are more likely to welcome your contributions, provide feedback, and help you grow as a contributor.

3. Start Small and Build Confidence

You don't need to jump into complex coding tasks immediately. Many open-source projects provide entry points for new contributors. Here are some simple ways to get started:

- Fix typos or errors in documentation
- Test and review open pull requests
- Work on issues labeled "good first issue," which are specifically chosen to help onboard new contributors
- Update outdated links or dependencies

Starting with smaller tasks helps you familiarize yourself with the project, its workflow, and the community. It also builds your confidence for tackling more significant contributions later.

4. **Organize Your Work on GitHub**

Once you start contributing, keeping your work organized is key. Create a GitHub profile that highlights your open-source activities, showcases your contributions, and demonstrates your growth over time. Use your profile as a living portfolio to connect with others and build your reputation in the open-source ecosystem.

STANDARDS

Standards are a technology backbone, enabling interoperability, consistency, and scalability across industries. They may not be as widely discussed as patents or copyrights, but they are among the most significant forms of IP. A standard is a documented agreement on how specific technologies or processes should work. These agreements are created collaboratively by industry leaders, researchers, and other stakeholders to ensure that products, systems, and services can function seamlessly.

Standards play a vital role in shaping the world we live in. From the Wi-Fi protocol that connects your devices to the TLS protocol that secures your online transactions, standards define the rules of the road for how technology operates. They are technical guidelines and powerful tools for driving innovation, fostering collaboration, and shaping the direction of entire industries.

Unlike patents, which grant exclusive rights to an invention, standards are typically open and collaborative. Contributing to standards establishes you as a thought leader and positions you as a committed community member. If done properly, it will also position your product as integration-friendly.

Contributing to standards is a powerful way to showcase your expertise. It is also a way to meet some amazing people. These efforts involve sharing specialized knowledge and insights often representing years of accumulated experience, research, and practical application. Standards documents explicitly list contributors, providing a permanent record of your role in their creation. This published acknowledgment demonstrates your depth of knowledge and reinforces your standing in the field. Additionally, being named as a contributor or leader in widely adopted standards cements your reputation as an authority, giving you recognition beyond your immediate organization.

When you participate in the development of standards, you gain the opportunity to shape the future of your industry. By contributing to or drafting them, you influence how technologies are adopted and implemented. This impact often dictates market trends and the evolution of entire sectors. Your work in standards leaves a legacy, as your contributions become embedded in how companies, governments, and organizations operate.

> By being part of standards development, you can provide unique contributions and see layers across different work streams that others might miss.
>
> —KATHLEEN MORIARTY

Standards development is inherently collaborative, involving diverse teams with varied expertise. While these efforts are team-based, individual contributions often stand out, showcasing your ability to collaborate while advancing your ideas. Participating in standards setting highlights your capacity to work across disciplines and build consensus. This visibility establishes you as a thought leader, driving innovation and fostering collective success. As Moriarty explains:

> It's not just about one area of expertise; it's about seeing across spaces and joining concepts for a bigger picture.
>
> —KATHLEEN MORIARTY

Active involvement in standards elevates your professional credibility, extending your influence beyond your role in a single organization. This industry-wide platform positions you as a trusted voice and a leader in your field. The recognition gained through standards work often opens doors to advisory boards, industry panels, and leadership roles within standards bodies. This pathway accelerates career growth and builds a network of professional connections that extends across the industry. By contributing to standards, you not only shape the future of technology, but also establish yourself as a leader who drives progress and innovation.

My experience in standards includes participating in the early OpenStack committee, small contributions in Kubernetes, and founding the CAT-MIP standard. I quickly learned that where there are committees, there is resistance. When entering the world of standards, you must be in it for the long haul and for a greater purpose. Moriarty points out the importance of persistence when facing resistance, saying:

> You have to believe in yourself and push for what you know is the right thing to do. The problem does need to be solved, and others may not fully grasp its scope.
>
> —KATHLEEN MORIARTY

Kathleen Moriarty's journey into the world of standards development was one of persistence, strategic learning, and a deeply ingrained sense of purpose. Recognizing early in her career that establishing standards was essential for the security and interoperability of systems and a powerful avenue for shaping the future of technology, Moriarty approached the field with both determination and humility.

Moriarty first immersed herself in the standards ecosystem, taking the time to understand the key players, processes, and politics involved. She realized that gaining influence in this space required more than technical expertise; it demanded building trust, demonstrating thought leadership, and contributing consistently to the greater good. Her ability to articulate the importance of security and ensure interoperability earned her respect within the community, but it was her patience and persistence that allowed her to navigate the often-bureaucratic systems that define standards organizations.

Moriarty focused on making strategic contributions. Rather than attempting to overhaul the system overnight, she identified critical areas where her expertise could make an immediate impact. Her deep technical knowledge of security protocols and her ability to translate complex ideas into actionable frameworks helped her gain credibility. Moriarty worked on smaller, manageable tasks at first, using these as stepping stones to larger, more influential projects. Each contribution built her reputation and solidified her standing within the standards community.

As her contributions accumulated, Moriarty leveraged her growing reputation to influence broader discussions within the field. She didn't shy away from leadership roles, taking on responsibilities that allowed her to guide the direction of standards development. Her work on security standards in particular became a cornerstone of her influence, showcasing her ability to balance technical precision with practical applicability.

Kathleen Moriarty's path into the world of standards demonstrates the power of perseverance, strategic action, and collaboration. Her journey serves as an inspiring blueprint for anyone looking to make an impact in a field where influence is earned through consistent effort and a commitment to the greater good.

How to Get Involved in Standards

1. **Choose the Right Committee:** Research standards organizations in your field, such as the IEEE, ISO, or IETF. Look for committees or working groups focused on areas relevant to your expertise.
2. **Be Collaborative:** Take part in joint discussions and draft reviews, and give feedback to others. As Moriarty shared,

> It takes persistence and trust in your expertise. Others may not always see the full scope of what you are doing, but that should not deter you from contributing.
>
> —KATHLEEN MORIARTY

   This mindset is crucial for making an impact.

3. **Bring Real-World Experience:** Standards benefit from practical insights. Share your day-to-day challenges and successes to ensure the standards being developed address real needs.
4. **Build Relationships:** Network with other participants to establish credibility and open doors for collaboration. Seek out an existing participant as a mentor—many are eager to support new talent and help them acclimate. Unlike traditional workplaces, standards forums foster deep, long-term

professional relationships, often spanning decades. While we engage in open debates with these colleagues, our shared goal is always to improve the quality of the work. Over time, consistent contributions can position you as a trusted voice in the community.

4

INTENTIONAL PURSUIT OF IP

To bring it all together, IP isn't something you stumble into. IP is strategic, deliberate, and, yes, a process-driven endeavor. And an IP portfolio is game-changing.

First, you need to make sure you have a personal plan to guide your actions. Next, you need to put the support structure in place to get there (which I do with mentor circles).

BUILD YOUR PERSONAL PLAN

By now, it should be clear that IP must be pursued intentionally. Each form of IP serves a distinct purpose; combining them can offer a robust protective strategy. For example, when developing new software or technology, you might use patents to protect underlying inventions; copyrights to safeguard source code and documentation, as well as other forms of content; trademarks to establish a recognizable brand; trade secrets to secure proprietary methods; open-source project contribution for complimentary technology; and standards establishment to ensure that products can work in the larger ecosystem. Each type of IP complements the others, creating a comprehensive framework for safeguarding and scaling innovation.

> If you stretch, you grow. That's been a consistent theme for me. I think about the problem set and my own experience, and come up with a protocol or approach that solves something critical.
>
> —KATHLEEN MORIARTY

Moriarty's approach highlights the importance of persistence and problem-solving; this is how she leveraged her own expertise to create IP that addresses critical gaps in technology and standards. Creating IP at scale requires intention and a methodical approach.

For Anne-Marie McReynolds, the key is to transform investigative superpowers into a framework for innovation:

> We look at user pain points and try to find those metrics, those KPIs, those markers that would translate to transparency and the ability to see in an explainable way why decisions were being made; and then intervene where the customer pain was too high.
>
> —ANNE-MARIE McREYNOLDS

Her ability to systematically identify and address pain points has driven her success in creating meaningful IP with major impact.

Will Allen brings a cross-disciplinary perspective to the table, pushing boundaries by finding new applications for existing technologies:

> If you're trying to create something disruptive, you've got to find the advantage you have and apply it to a completely new arena. It's

> about identifying where you can solve real problems in adjacent or even unrelated spaces.
>
> —WILL ALLEN

Allen's strategy shows how leveraging expertise across domains enables disruptive innovation and the creation of highly effective IP.

IP is a strategy for professional and organizational growth, influence, and impact—and like any strategy, it works best when approached with clarity, focus, and a determination to create value. To get from concept to creation, you need to build a plan and a roadmap that helps you stay focused and productive along the way. Let's dive into how you can craft a plan to pursue IP and take your ideas from spark to substance.

1. OUTLINE YOUR STRATEGIC OBJECTIVES Take a step back and think about why you're doing this. Where are you in your career journey? What are your strategic objectives? Are you looking to grow your technical expertise? Do you want to learn new skills, or is your primary goal to secure a promotion by demonstrating measurable contributions to your company or in an industry? Are you looking to collaborate? To influence the industry? Perhaps you're even eyeing external recognition as a thought leader in your field. Whatever your goals are, be specific and clear. There is a great step-by-step plan in appendix C to help you get started.

2. LOOK AT YOUR INDUSTRY: WHAT'S INTERESTING, AND WHAT PROBLEMS NEED SOLVING? Once your objectives are clear, it's time to look outward toward your industry. What are the hot topics, and what gaps exist? The best IP stems from identifying a problem that hasn't been solved or hasn't been solved well. To do this, you need to keep your ear to the ground: regularly read industry reports, attend webinars, listen to podcasts, and engage in professional forums. What are people struggling with? Look at other vendors and partners in your industry. Where are they headed, what do their keynotes talk about, and what do you see for strategic direction in their SEC filings?

What are the emerging technologies, methodologies, or trends? By understanding what's happening in your field, you'll find inspiration and ensure your IP is relevant and timely. Revisit the problem identification section.

3. IDENTIFY INTERNAL OPPORTUNITIES Now, let's look inward: your company is full of opportunities for IP creation; you just have to know where to find them. What are your organization's strategic objectives? Where are they investing, and what new products, services, or technologies are they building? Companies often have unaddressed problems or overlooked processes that are ripe for innovation. If you are in a position to talk to your customers, do so and ask for their thoughts. Nobody can tell you what the problems are better than the people who are experiencing them directly. Perhaps a customer has a recurring issue, or maybe a product could benefit from a new feature that you've been thinking about for a while—these are all opportunities for you to create something new and valuable.

You also want to identify what IP resources you already have. Does your company offer support for patent filings or provide access to legal teams who can help refine your ideas? Do they have initiatives where employees can contribute to company blogs or speak on their behalf? Find your internal public relations (PR) team and take them to lunch. In general, building relationships and helping the agenda of internal resources is key, and PR typically has their fingers on the pulse of the organization and goals. Some organizations even offer bonuses or incentives for employees who successfully file patents or create IP. By aligning your IP goals with your company's strategic direction, you increase the likelihood of creating something that benefits you and the business.

4. IDENTIFY EXTERNAL OPPORTUNITIES While your internal opportunities are valuable, look toward external channels that can amplify your efforts. Conferences, industry standards groups, and professional societies offer platforms for you to publish your work, present innovative ideas, and gain recognition. Get your name out there *and* connect with people. Collaboration and external visibility significantly increase the likelihood of getting your ideas recognized and published.

Look at conferences where you'd like to speak. What are the submission deadlines? What types of papers are typically accepted? Consider professional societies that support IP development in your field, such as the Institute of Electrical and Electronics Engineers (IEEE). These organizations often offer mentorship, peer reviews, and platforms to showcase your work.

5. SET IP CREATION GOALS AND TIMELINES One of the most essential steps in pursuing IP is deciding how much IP you want to create and by when. You can't control whether a patent gets approved, a standard gets adopted, or a code submission is merged. However, you can control how many ideas you develop and submit; the same goes for publications, conference appearances, or any other IP-related goals. A good starting point is to set specific, measurable goals like, "I will write and submit five patent applications in the next twelve months," or "I will publish two peer-reviewed articles and present at one conference this year." Choose realistic goals that fit your workload and other professional commitments.

6. BUILD A SCHEDULE IP creation is not inspiration-driven; it is process-driven. You need to set aside regular, dedicated time for IP work, whether that's brainstorming, writing code, reviewing standards, or writing articles. One of the best ways to ensure you stay on track is to build a consistent schedule. Block out time on your calendar each week for IP-related tasks, even if it's just an hour.

7. MEASURE, ADAPT, AND IMPROVE Just because you made your goals doesn't mean the plan is set in stone. Be prepared to measure your progress and adjust if necessary. If you're not hitting your targets, ask yourself why. Do you need more time, different resources, or additional support? Evaluate your progress regularly, and if specific strategies aren't working, pivot and try new approaches. Flexibility is key to long-term success.

And don't go it alone. If you are not currently participating in mentor circles or affinity groups, consider the next section. You can easily set these up, and they will propel your success.

BUILD YOUR SUPPORT SYSTEM

Mentor circles, also referred to as affinity groups or peer groups, have been a geometric growth factor in my IP career. If you're unfamiliar with the concept, a mentor circle is a focused group of individuals with a shared goal or interest. These groups commit to meeting regularly over a set period to support each other's growth. I have been part of, and have also started, several that are centered around IP generation. This has directly led to patents, publications, speaking engagements, and more. A mentor circle connection led directly to a webinar on the topic of IP as well as appendix C with Noell Ochieng. I strongly advise you to join one, or even start one of your own.

What sets mentor circles apart is their ability to function as incubators for innovation, collaboration, and career advancement. By fostering open dialogue, embracing diverse perspectives, and maintaining accountability, these circles create a supportive yet structured environment where participants achieve their goals and develop essential skills.

Unlike traditional one-on-one mentoring, mentor circles leverage the collective wisdom of the group, offering rich, multidimensional perspectives on professional challenges and opportunities. The group typically combines one-on-one peer sessions with full group discussions, allowing members to tackle goals, refine skills, and expand their networks.

The inclusive and collaborative nature of mentor circles makes them uniquely effective for cultivating IP. They provide a safe space for brainstorming, refining ideas, and gaining constructive feedback—all key ingredients for innovation. Whether your focus is on patents, open-source contributions, or building thought leadership, a mentor circle can transform your ideas into tangible results.

> The magic happens when the team is better than the problem. When you bring together people with shared passions and complementary skills, the collective energy can tackle challenges that feel insurmountable alone. Affinity groups naturally amplify collaboration, build trust, and unlock creativity.
>
> —WILL ALLEN

Affinity is the cornerstone of successful mentor circles. Shared interests and goals create a foundation of trust, enabling participants to collaborate effectively and share vulnerabilities without fear of judgment. When people feel aligned in purpose, they are more likely to take risks, offer candid feedback, and work together to overcome obstacles.

I have set up and run mentor circles at multiple companies, including Dell, Iron Mountain, and N-able, and there are a few ingredients you need to think through when pulling them together. Trust is the cornerstone, diversity is necessary, everyone must be accountable, and feedback is key. Together these create momentum.

In small groups with a shared affinity, whether technical or otherwise, trust is built more quickly and deeply than in larger settings. This trust enables participants to share openly (whether it's innovative ideas, professional struggles, or aspirations) without fear of judgment. As you lean into this vulnerability, you create an environment where others feel safe doing the same, fostering a culture of authenticity and growth.

When forming the circles, I first consider the affinity I am interested in—technology, professional role, or something else? Then, look for people from diverse backgrounds with the same interest. Diversity, in this case, can be schooling, the way people think, geographic location, problem-solving skills, or job experiences. When you're surrounded by people who approach challenges differently, you're exposed to new ways of thinking that can inspire breakthrough ideas. By actively engaging with diverse viewpoints, you stretch your own thinking and open doors to solutions you might never have considered on your own.

These groups are structured and have meeting schedules; this drives accountability, which then drives results. This structure helps you stay focused and motivated to deliver on your commitments, knowing others are invested in your success. The simple act of articulating your goals to the group makes them more real and actionable.

One of the added benefits of mentor circles is the opportunity to receive and provide feedback in a constructive, supportive setting. By presenting your ideas, whether it's a pitch, a patent concept, or a personal challenge, you gain insights from people who want to see you succeed. Constructive feedback sharpens your ideas, eliminates blind spots, and strengthens your confidence to act.

Finally, momentum is contagious. In a well-functioning mentor circle, the energy of progress feeds itself. When one person shares a win, it inspires others to push harder toward their own goals. The shared celebration of success, no matter how small, reinforces the value of the circle and builds momentum for everyone involved.

To leverage these dynamics, approach your mentor circle with intentionality. Be clear about your goals, actively listen to others, and contribute generously. Invest in the relationships you're building because the value of a mentor circle extends far beyond its formal meetings. You can create a network of advocates and collaborators, all of whom amplify others' potential.

The Structure of a Mentor Circle

An effective mentor circle thrives on structure and purpose, particularly when the focus is on generating IP. To create one, start by forming a small, intentional group of four to six individuals who share a commitment to innovation and IP. I often create a form and send it to a large number of individuals so that people can opt in if they are interested in a topic. This opt-in increases the likelihood that participants are interested and committed.

At N-able, we determined that there was a lack of mentoring opportunities for women. In 2024, I founded and led the first mentor circles with amazing peers from all over the globe. I built small groups of team members, being sure to include team members from different physical locations, different teams, and with different years of experience.

When you have selected a set of circle members, begin with a whole group kickoff session where participants introduce themselves and outline their interests and goals related to IP creation. During this session, members articulate specific objectives, such as identifying patentable ideas, refining open-source contributions, or building thought leadership through publications. The kickoff sets the tone for the circle by emphasizing collaborative learning, shared accountability, and a focus on actionable results.

Over the course of the cycle, participants engage in weekly one-on-one meetings. These confidential discussions allow members to dive deeply into their ideas, challenges, and progress. By rotating partners each week, members gain fresh perspectives and tailored feedback, which often sparks innovative approaches. These conversations are pivotal for identifying unique solutions to pressing challenges and uncovering the seeds of patentable concepts.

At scheduled intervals, the circle reconvenes for group sessions. These meetings are where individual insights are synthesized into collective breakthroughs. Members share progress, reflect on feedback from their one-on-one conversations, and evaluate ideas against criteria for patentability, open-source value, or thought leadership potential. Together, the group refines concepts, identifies next steps, and sets priorities for moving forward. These sessions foster collaboration and build momentum by celebrating progress and aligning on strategic goals.

The cycle repeats over several months, with each iteration offering opportunities to set new goals, address emerging challenges, and build on previous successes. At the conclusion of the second cycle, the circle dissolves, allowing members to take their refined ideas and strengthened relationships into new opportunities for IP creation and career advancement.

By maintaining a balance of individual focus and group collaboration, this structure ensures high engagement and accountability. Each participant has the opportunity to contribute their unique strengths while benefiting from the collective wisdom of the group. This model accelerates the creation of IP and builds lasting networks of advocates and collaborators, amplifying the impact of everyone involved.

Whether you're contributing to open source, developing patents, or exploring new ideas, mentor circles offer a robust framework for turning ambition into achievement. Start your circle today and unlock the full potential of collaborative IP creation.

5

THE ROLE OF GENERATIVE AI IN CREATING IP

The rise of generative AI, such as ChatGPT, Claude, or Copilot, has introduced a new tool that can assist in the IP generation process. However, like all tools, it must be used thoughtfully and strategically. Generative AI is not a replacement for expertise (as people sometimes think); instead, it's an augmentative tool to help you refine, explore, and shape your ideas. Used correctly, it can accelerate your IP creation process. Used carelessly, it can derail your credibility and even land you in legal trouble.

HOW GENERATIVE AI WORKS

Generative AI is designed to process vast amounts of data, identify patterns, and use those patterns to create new outputs with variation. It operates by following rules and models it has been trained on, applying these learned patterns to new inputs. This makes it exceptionally skilled at tasks like summarizing, brainstorming, and refining content. However, generative AI does not reason or think independently. Instead, it synthesizes and extrapolates based on the patterns it has been exposed to during training.

At the heart of such AI is a neural network architecture, typically a transformer model, trained on extensive datasets. These datasets span a wide variety of domains, enabling the AI to simulate humanlike responses and assist in various creative and technical processes. Tools like ChatGPT and GitHub Copilot harness these capabilities to support brainstorming, coding, and writing tasks.

Generative AI can be an invaluable partner in the intellectual property (IP) creation process, helping you refine ideas, structure content, and explore possibilities efficiently. For example:

- Writing and Editing: If you are drafting a patent application or article, AI can suggest ways to improve grammar, clarity, or structure, helping you produce polished, professional results.
- Research Assistance: AI tools can quickly summarize related concepts or innovations, providing a starting point for deeper investigation.
- Coding and Prototyping: GitHub Copilot can suggest boilerplate code or offer solutions for debugging, accelerating your workflow and freeing you to focus on more complex challenges.

Imagine you are drafting a patent and struggling with the technical description of an innovative feature; generative AI could help refine your language, ensuring it is both clear and precise. Or perhaps you need to identify gaps in existing patents or standards: by asking targeted questions, AI can surface relevant information in minutes, saving you hours of manual research.

While generative AI excels at finding and recreating patterns, it is not capable of independent reasoning or true innovation.

It works within the confines of its training data and does not understand the nuanced complexities of your field. This means that while it can assist in refining and synthesizing information, the creative breakthroughs come from you.

Generative AI cannot ensure originality, accuracy, realness, or verify that its outputs do not overlap with existing protected IP. To maximize its usefulness, always review and validate its outputs. Cross-reference its suggestions with trusted sources, especially when working on technical or highly specific content.

Generative AI is a powerful tool, but its value lies in complementing your creativity and expertise. By understanding its strengths and limitations, you can harness its capabilities to streamline your work and focus on developing ideas and solutions that drive innovation.

THE LIMITS OF GENERATIVE AI IN IP CREATION

IP, *by definition*, requires the creation of something novel, something that has not existed before. AI can assist you in that journey, but the end result is highly questionable if you have it take the lead.

One of the most common mistakes I've seen is people relying too heavily on generative AI to create an entire patent or article from scratch. The technology may give you a starting point or offer useful suggestions, but if you try to let AI do all the work you'll end up with something generic, often riddled with inaccuracies, and devoid of true innovation.

This is where the danger of AI hallucinations comes into play. Generative AI sometimes produces information that sounds plausible but is factually incorrect—or entirely fabricated. The accuracy rating of new LLMs and models released in 2025—within contexts where they are trained—is estimated to range from 70 to 90 percent. This means that as you interact with the tools and build out articles and patents, between 10 and 30 percent of the information you get back is likely to be inaccurate. While this is continually improving, if you do not know enough about a topic to find that 10 to 30 percent and fix it, you should not be using GenAI to write the content. This can be especially problematic when you're working on a patent, where accuracy and originality are paramount. Imagine submitting a patent application only to realize that the AI-created text contains faulty information, or worse, that it inadvertently mirrors existing technology too closely. The resulting patent could be rejected and could harm your reputation as an innovator.

When using AI, you must always ask for attribution: always ask the AI to supply you with sources for the information it provides. If it returns a reference article, you must check that the article actually exists and that its content is accurately represented. Just as you would double-check an article you read in a magazine or academic journal, you need to verify anything generated by AI. If the software suggests that your innovation overlaps with existing tech, ask for links to those sources so you can review them yourself. This ensures that you're not accidentally infringing on someone else's IP or building your innovation on incorrect data.

USE AI TO AUGMENT, NOT REPLACE, YOUR EXPERTISE

Generative AI should not replace the deep learning, critical thinking, and industry-specific knowledge that you've worked hard to develop. IP comes from your understanding of your field, your ability to see patterns others miss, and your knack for turning those insights into something new.

For example, I use AI to help refine language or offer structural suggestions for articles. At the end of the day, the core ideas, the innovation itself, come from my customer interactions, my mind, and my experiences. While AI might help me clean up the language of my patent filing, I do not use it to dream up the solution to a complex problem. That's where human expertise shines—and it's the part of the entire process that gives me the spark of joy. Why would I give that up?! AI, when used properly, can accelerate the process and free up more of your time for high-level thinking. It helps you focus on what matters most—innovating.

If you use AI, be smart about it. You must maintain your ethical standards and ensure that your work remains grounded in verifiable sources; this practice upholds the integrity of your IP and helps establish trust within your industry.

AI LEGAL CONSIDERATIONS AND COPYRIGHT IMPLICATIONS

Generative AI relies on massive datasets that may include copyrighted material. While the AI itself may not directly infringe on these rights, you could face legal issues if your IP borrows too heavily from preexisting works.

At the time of writing, legislation in the United States is still in flux. However, recent legislation, such as the European Union AI Act (EU AI Act), has introduced stricter guidelines for how AI interacts with copyrighted content. These laws are complex, evolving, and vary by jurisdiction, making it essential to stay informed. The key takeaway is clear: it is your responsibility to ensure your IP does not inadvertently infringe on copyright protections. The potential legal and reputational consequences are too significant to ignore.

To safeguard your work, avoid feeding AI systems content that includes copyrighted material unless you have explicit permission to use it. Keep your innovations original and ensure that AI serves as a support tool, helping you refine and accelerate your ideas rather than generating them outright.

Generative AI, when used responsibly, can enhance your ability to create IP. However, the expertise, creativity, and originality required to innovate must remain your own. By carefully checking AI-generated content for accuracy and originality, staying informed about legal developments, and ensuring proper citation when needed, you can integrate AI into your IP creation strategy effectively and safely. The future of innovation is promising, but only when we use AI tools with care and intention.

6

LEVERAGING IP FOR PROFESSIONAL GROWTH

When you're building a career, you also need to develop your personal brand. Think of your personal brand as the sum total of how people perceive you, your expertise, and the value you bring to the table. It's what makes you come to mind when a new role opens up, what makes a potential partner reach out for collaboration, and what gets you invited to industry conversations.

Being a decent, reliable, and hard-working person who is knowledgeable in your field is a baseline requirement if you wish to work with other people. So please, do not neglect those aspects, but that is a completely different set of content better covered by Brene Brown and Adam Grant. Building strong credentials through the generation of IP serves as one foundation of your brand.

IP speaks for you when you're not in the room, but—herein lies the rub—it can only speak for you if other people know about your IP. As you accumulate credentials, you need to disclose them. And if you walk the line effectively, you'll find that creating awareness of your work opens doors. Internally, it might lead to new roles or promotions; externally, it can attract job offers, speaking engagements, and opportunities to sit on boards. This creates a flywheel of incredible opportunities.

> IP gives you some data that's non-negotiable, that no one can take away from you. It makes people see you differently. It gives you the power to move—whether within your current organization or into a new role—and builds confidence in your communication to articulate your value.
>
> —ANNE-MARIE McREYNOLDS

This advice highlights how IP serves as a tangible, permanent record of your contributions, making it easier for others to recognize and appreciate your expertise. It is a way of saying, "*This is what I've created, and it matters.*" IP not only enhances your personal brand but also shifts how others perceive and evaluate your contributions, opening doors to new opportunities.

McReynolds's insight emphasizes that IP is more than a career milestone; it is a confidence-building tool. When you can point to a patent, a copyright, or a significant contribution to standards, you have concrete evidence of your impact. This shifts the narrative around your expertise from subjective to objective, allowing you to communicate your value more effectively. Whether you are seeking a promotion, exploring a new role, or building thought leadership in your industry, IP becomes a foundation for self-assurance and credibility.

Beyond personal branding, IP allows you to navigate your career with greater freedom; it is something that cannot be taken away. It provides leverage in negotiations and opens pathways to roles where your contributions will be valued. It transforms how you are perceived, positioning you not just as a participant but as a leader and innovator in your field. By creating and leveraging IP, you take control of your narrative, shaping how others see you.

POSITIONING YOUR ACCOMPLISHMENTS

How do you cut through personal biases, office politics, and subjective evaluations? Merely having IP isn't enough. You have to leverage it correctly to unlock doors and ensure your contributions are recognized. IP is a list of achievements, yes, *and* it's the story of your growth, influence, and impact. Whether you're leveraging patents, trade secrets, copyrights, trademarks, open source, or standards, IP narrates your journey from inventing solutions to innovating within teams and, ultimately, influencing your industry.

Defining Your Unique Value Proposition

Many people struggle with self-promotion, especially if they are not naturally inclined to talk about their accomplishments. It is an uncomfortable truth that the loudest voices often get noticed first, but you do not need to be loud to be effective. Instead of thinking about self-promotion as bragging, consider it an opportunity to share with others. When you share your knowledge, you are not boasting. You are providing value.

> You can't just do good work and hope it gets recognized. You need to create artifacts—proof of what you've done, like patents or publications—to position yourself.
>
> —WILL ALLEN

Self-promotion, when reframed as teaching or providing value, is not boastful—it is essential. Many people shy away from advocating for themselves because they perceive it as arrogance, but as Allen notes, simply doing good work is not enough to ensure recognition or advancement in competitive or hierarchical environments.

Creating "artifacts" such as patents, publications, or other tangible proof of your contributions ensures that your work is visible, measurable, and makes an impact. These artifacts do more than highlight what you've accomplished; they teach, inspire, and guide others. They become tools for demonstrating your expertise and extending your influence without requiring you to promote yourself directly.

When you think of creating artifacts as sharing knowledge, it shifts the purpose from self-promotion to contributing to a broader community. Patents, for example, showcase innovative problem-solving and encourage others to think in new ways. Publications allow you to share your insights and expertise, offering practical guidance or sparking fresh ideas in your field. Open-source contributions quite literally move the community forward through code contributions.

In standards work, one way to share knowledge is by contributing to others' efforts. This can include reviewing drafts that may not be directly relevant to your work but are related enough that your input adds value; even identifying a technical or grammatical error is helpful. Additionally, voicing support for someone else's work can be valuable, especially if a commenter lacks the perspective to fully understand its importance. Engaging in these ways strengthens the community and fosters collaboration.

> When I realized I wasn't advancing, I began thinking long-term, leaving artifacts, and pushing for visibility of my contributions.
>
> —WILL ALLEN

This highlights a pivotal shift in mindset. Instead of waiting for recognition, Allen took control of his narrative by creating lasting, tangible evidence of his work. Artifacts like patents and publications serve as milestones that showcase not only technical expertise but also the ability to address real-world challenges.

Thinking long-term means identifying ways your contributions align with broader business goals and documenting them in ways that endure. For Allen, this strategy wasn't just about personal success; it was about creating a legacy of impactful work that others could reference and build upon. By leaving artifacts, you make your value visible in a way that transcends day-to-day interactions, ensuring your efforts contribute to both individual and organizational growth.

This approach is compelling in environments where systemic biases or hierarchical structures make it challenging to stand out. Artifacts provide an objective record of your achievements, making it easier for others to recognize and advocate for your contributions.

Artifacts not only advance your career, but also serve as powerful tools for teaching and mentoring. They bring value to your professional environment by fostering collaboration and innovation. Allen's insight shows us how important it is to create visible and lasting evidence of our work. Let your work speak for itself in a way that resonates and matters.

> Teaching first-time inventors how to file patents empowers them with tangible proof of their value. It's about overcoming exclusion and gaining recognition.
>
> —ANNE-MARIE McREYNOLDS

This statement underscores the importance of IP as a tool for visibility and equity. Without deliberate promotion, even the most groundbreaking inventions risk being overlooked.

Promoting your IP helps your contributions get recognized and can be leveraged to foster growth, inclusivity, and collaboration. Consider the Mentor Circles outlined in chapter 4: these drew in participants because they were able to see the success of others. McReynolds reinforces the notion that visibility doesn't happen by accident. Artifacts like patents and papers serve as tangible markers of your value, helping others understand and appreciate your work.

As I mentioned previously, many people struggle with self-promotion because they equate it with arrogance or self-aggrandizement. Promotion doesn't have to feel self-serving. When you share your work, you're providing value to others by teaching, inspiring, or guiding them.

IP plays a key role in establishing credibility. Your IP serves as tangible evidence of your ability to create something new, whether it is solving customer problems, developing innovative processes, or generating new ideas. Use your IP to show that you are a creator and a thinker who actively contributes to the growth of your organization or industry. Highlight the specific value you have added. For example, if you have filed a patent through the USPTO website, do not just mention the filing. Explain how the idea behind the patent saved your company money, improved efficiency, or opened new revenue streams. This transforms your IP from a simple bullet point on your resume into a strategic asset that demonstrates your problem-solving skills and innovative mindset, and it promotes your company as innovative.

IP gives you the opportunity to showcase your creativity and the value you bring. It positions you as someone who actively contributes to organizational growth and aligns your achievements with the goals of your company or industry. By being specific and intentional about how you present your IP, you can ensure it reflects your unique value proposition and strengthens your professional reputation.

Once you've established your value, position yourself as a collaborative innovator. Shift the narrative to show how your IP contributions have enabled shared success. You can achieve this shift by leading a cross-functional team to develop a new product or coauthoring a technical paper that paves the way for future innovations.

We will review specific ways to do this in just a minute, but first, I want to discuss why you don't want to do this alone.

Collaborating to Create Bigger Impact

IP will become a bridge to the next level of your career if you talk about how your work has empowered your team, solved challenges, and contributed to larger business objectives. When you frame your accomplishments in this way, you're demonstrating leadership and an ability to elevate those around you.

> I connect ideas and people, creating thought leadership that not only informs, but catalyzes, action. You don't have to call yourself a thought leader—your work will show it.
>
> —BILL PFEIFER

This insight reinforces the idea that thought leadership (as discussed in chapter 3) is not self-proclaimed; it emerges naturally when your contributions resonate with and inspire others. When you show how your IP solves problems, facilitates collaboration, and drives meaningful change, you amplify its impact and demonstrate authentic leadership.

> I did not benefit from external blog posts or writing books . . . until blogging became recognized as a competitive advantage. Writing differentiated me and ended up being great for my career.
>
> —STEVE TODD

Blogging about his innovations helped Todd to stand out, while helping others understand the creative process behind his successful products. And ultimately, it helped his company. Sharing your IP is less about saying, "Look what I did," and more about saying, "Here's how this could help."

> Networking and collaboration were key to my success . . . The promotions that brought me to the highest levels as a software engineer were a direct result of writing externally and publicly.
>
> —STEVE TODD

By sharing his insights through blog posts, white papers, and public speaking, Todd positioned himself as a thought leader who could connect ideas and drive industry-wide conversations.

Sharing credit is crucial here. It shows humility and that you are invested in your team's success. As noted in chapter one, Henry Chesbrough's Open Innovation model points out that breakthrough ideas often come from external sources. Showing that you collaborated effectively with others, whether internally or across organizations, demonstrates that you are someone who fosters a culture of innovation. This ability to collaborate and bring out the best in others is a key differentiator when positioning yourself for leadership roles.

Using IP to Lead and Shape the Industry

As you reach the later stages of your career, the focus shifts from personal and team achievements to industry influence. At this stage, your IP is not just a record of what you've done; it's a platform for you to influence and inspire change across the broader industry.

At this level, recognize that IP isn't just a credential—it's a voice. It's your way of saying, "This is how I've contributed to advancing my industry." Your IP portfolio becomes a legacy. By positioning your IP this way, you're demonstrating that your influence extends far beyond your organization, making you indispensable not only to a single company but to an entire sector. And influence begets influence.

Kathleen Moriarty offers another perspective, stating:

> When I moved to being independent, I realized no one can say no anymore . . . We're sometimes stifled by others' opinions, but if you break free, you can do more.
>
> —KATHLEEN MORIARTY

Her sentiment captures the transformative power of taking ownership of your narrative and contributions. By stepping outside the constraints of traditional roles, Moriarty used her expertise to challenge norms and shape systemic change.

Using IP to shape the industry requires a proactive approach:

- **Public Sharing:** Publish your findings, ideas, and innovations in forums that reach beyond your immediate organization. By contributing to industry journals, conferences, or blogs, you establish yourself as a credible voice in your field.

- **Fostering Collaboration:** Leverage your IP to create opportunities for cross-industry partnerships. For example, a well-documented standard could serve as the foundation for a collaborative project between companies.
- **Addressing Systemic Challenges:** Use your platform to advocate for broader changes, whether through setting new standards, influencing policy, or championing ethical practices.
- **Mentoring the Next Generation:** Share your knowledge and experience with upcoming professionals, ensuring that your influence continues to ripple outward.

By using your IP to lead and shape the industry, you move from being a contributor to a catalyst for change. Your work becomes the foundation for innovations that extend far beyond your own achievements. A few years ago, I had an idea. I suspected that customers would be willing to shift the location of their hosted cloud resources if they understood the environmental impact of their choices. Imagine selecting a data center powered entirely by solar energy instead of one fueled by coal and being able to see the difference in emissions quantified in real time. From my years working in the energy efficiency market, I knew that measuring this type of information was absolutely possible. I believed that if we made sustainability visible, customers would make more responsible choices. At the time, the idea had no internal support. I was told, bluntly, that customers cared only about cost and performance. Still, I gathered a small group of like-minded colleagues to formalize the concept, and together we filed a series of patents. I started writing blogs and articles about it and even gave a talk at Dell Tech World on the topic. What I was told no one would be interested in has taken on a life of its own. And the baseline sustainability metrics have been wildly expanded and live on as a feature in a major vendor's cloud platform.

At every stage, the key to positioning your accomplishments is to craft a strategic narrative around your personal brand through the use of IP. This is weaving a story of growth, collaboration, and influence that shows how your work has evolved and contributed to the success of teams, organizations, and industries.

By framing your IP, you create a compelling story of professional growth and impact—one that positions you for promotion and long-term industry leadership.

How to Promote Your IP Effectively

1. **Start with Artifacts:** Begin by creating IP that is both meaningful and tangible. Put pen to paper (or screen)—literally—so there is a physical or digital object you can point to. Patents, publications, open-source contributions, standards, and presentations serve as clear evidence of your expertise and contributions. Whether it's a new product design, a research paper, or a trademarked brand, make sure your IP is well-documented and aligns with your professional goals.
2. **Build Narratives Around Your Work:** Don't just present your IP; tell the story behind it. What problem did it solve? What was your inspiration? How does it impact your industry? By framing your contributions as part of a larger narrative, you make them more relatable and engaging. Refer to the Thought Leadership section for ideas on how to tell a story. I love to use journey maps and storyboards to make this communication clear. Consider creating a wireframe or low-resolution prototype to help others really understand your vision and contributions.

3. **Leverage Multiple Platforms:** Choose the right platforms to share your work. Blog posts, LinkedIn articles, conference presentations, podcasts, and academic journals are just a few options. Tailor your approach to your audience. For example, a technical audience may prefer detailed white papers, while concise presentations might resonate more with business stakeholders.
4. **Teach and Mentor:** One of the most powerful ways to promote your IP is by teaching others how to create their own. McReynolds's philosophy of mentoring first-time inventors ensures that her influence extends beyond her individual contributions. By sharing your knowledge and guiding others, you not only expand your impact but also position yourself as a thought leader.
5. **Engage with the Community:** Collaboration is a multiplier for visibility. Join professional groups, attend industry events, and participate in panels or workshops. Sharing your insights in these spaces will increase your exposure and help you build valuable relationships.
6. **Focus on Value Over Volume:** Quality is better than quantity when promoting IP. A single, well-crafted article or presentation shared many times can have more impact than a dozen generic artifacts. Focus on delivering clear, actionable insights your peers will remember and share.

FRAMING IP FOR NEW POSITIONS OR PROMOTIONS

When asking for a promotion or applying for a new job, IP enables you to demonstrate tangible accomplishments that are indisputable regardless of personal biases or office politics.

When I realized that many promotion criteria were subjective, such as "being respected by peers" or "influencing a product," I zeroed in on IP to prove my promotion worthiness.

In my experience, securing a promotion was much easier when I had publications, speaking references, and patents to back me up. A key advantage is that they are quantifiable: either you have them, or you don't. In most organizations, the promotion or review cycle offers the opportunity to outline your accomplishments in terms of quality and quantity; IP can fit both metrics. When you've created IP, it's important to strategically position those accomplishments in a way that highlights what you did, why it matters, and the impact it has on the business. Below are examples of how to present various types of IP to support a promotion.

Patents: Demonstrating Innovation and Business Value

When you're aiming for a promotion or applying for a new job, you can't control how others perceive your influence or reputation. But you can control the number of patents you submit and the quality of the innovations they represent. Assembling this portfolio creates a strong, objective case for why you deserve to advance to the next level.

When outlining a patent's significance, focus on how your invention solved a problem, contributed to a product or service, and drove measurable business impact.

For example:

What I did: I developed and patented a fault-tolerant cloud infrastructure solution that enables reliable and scalable enterprise applications.

Why it matters: This patent addresses a key issue in cloud computing, which is reducing downtime and increasing service availability, both of which are critical for business continuity in modern cloud environments.

Impact on the business: This innovation directly contributed to the cloud offerings by enabling higher uptime guarantees, which led to increased customer trust and new enterprise-level contracts.

This format highlights your technical contribution while tying it to the company's overall business strategy. It explains what you invented and how it pushed the business forward.

Trade Secrets: Securing Competitive Advantage

Unlike patents or trademarks, trade secrets are not publicly disclosed. When highlighting trade secrets, emphasize the strategic advantage they offer the company and how you played a role in protecting or leveraging this knowledge without violating your employer's secrets.

For example:

What I did: I developed and maintained a proprietary algorithm for optimizing data storage across hybrid cloud environments, which is treated as a trade secret.

Why it matters: The algorithm significantly reduces costs for large-scale data storage and retrieval, a major pain point for enterprise customers. Keeping this solution confidential ensures that competitors cannot replicate our advantage in this space.

Impact on the business: This trade secret has been a key differentiator in Company Name's cloud services, contributing to a

30 percent reduction in operational costs for clients and boosting long-term customer retention.

You are positioning your work as a meaningful, behind-the-scenes contribution to the company's success.

Copyrights: Establishing Thought Leadership

I have the most copyright experience with publications. This form of IP typically demonstrates thought leadership. When discussing publications, focus on how they contributed to your personal brand as an industry expert and how they positioned your company in the market.

For example:

What I did: I published a paper on AI ethics and data transparency, outlining best practices for reducing bias in machine learning algorithms.

Why it matters: As AI continues to integrate into everyday business operations, ethical concerns around transparency and bias have become key issues within the industry and in our customer base. My work contributes to shaping the ethical standards that will guide the future of AI deployment in the industry.

Impact on the business: By establishing Company Name as a thought leader in AI ethics, my publication attracted attention of key clients and partners in the technology space, leading to new business opportunities and enhancing the company's reputation for responsible AI development. The paper has had sizeable reach: 3,400 social media impressions when posted by me on LinkedIn, 10,900+ downloads from the CompanyName.com website, and the basis for twelve Company Name social posts.

In this case, the focus is on the external influence your work has, both for yourself as a leader and for your organization.

Trademarks: Protecting Brand and Market Identity

Trademarks protect the symbols, names, and branding of your products and services. In a promotion context, you would highlight how trademarks have strengthened brand recognition and protected market share.

For example:

What I did: I led the creation and trademarking of a new brand for a cloud-based AI service under Company Name's offerings.

Why it matters: The trademark helps Company Name protect its market identity in the rapidly growing AI-as-a-service space, ensuring that no other competitors can capitalize on the brand equity we are building.

Impact on the business: The trademarked brand has been pivotal in launching new AI products and correlates with a 20 percent increase in market share in the cloud services sector.

By explaining how you protected and elevated your company's brand through IP, you showcase your understanding of both technical and business strategy.

Open-Source Contributions: A Differentiator

Contributing to open source is one of the most effective ways to demonstrate technical expertise, collaboration, and influence. Open-source contributions not only showcase your ability to create impactful solutions but also position you and your organization as leaders in fostering innovation and transparency.

For example:

What I did: I contributed a new module to a widely used open-source project using Python, Java, and writing documentation, thus enhancing its capabilities for cloud security.

Why it matters: By improving a widely used tool, we enabled thousands of users to implement stronger security protocols.

Impact on the business: This contribution positioned Company Name as a leader in the open-source community, increasing brand visibility among developers and potential partners. The module has been downloaded 50,000+ times, with fifteen companies integrating it into their solutions. This visibility has opened doors to partnerships, new hires, and speaking engagements, further establishing the company's influence in the cloud security space.

In this case, the focus is on how your open-source contributions differentiate you and your organization by highlighting technical skills, collaborative spirit, and the ability to solve real-world problems at scale. By framing your work in this way, you demonstrate leadership and a deep commitment to advancing both technology and community.

Standards: Establishing Industry Benchmarks

Creating and contributing to standards is a strategic way to demonstrate leadership and shape the direction of your industry.

Standards ensure interoperability, foster innovation, and establish trust among industry stakeholders.

What I did: I contributed to an industry-wide standard for secure data transmission protocols in cloud environments, collaborating with peers from leading organizations and regulatory bodies.

Why it matters: Standards are the foundation of scalable, reliable, and interoperable systems. By contributing to this standard, I ensured that organizations across the globe could securely manage and exchange data, addressing a critical industry need.

Impact on the business: Establishing this standard positioned Company Name as a trusted authority in cloud security. It opened opportunities to influence policy decisions, secure strategic partnerships, and expand into new markets. Additionally, our involvement in creating the standard strengthened relationships with regulatory bodies, enhancing our reputation as a responsible and forward-thinking organization.

Contributing to standards is more than technical expertise; you must set the stage for future innovation and ensure that your organization plays a key role in defining what's next for your industry. By framing your work this way, you position yourself as a thought leader driving progress and creating a legacy of impact.

When presenting IP achievements in promotion discussions, the key is to frame each accomplishment within the broader context of business strategy and impact. By showing what you did and why it matters to the organization, you provide concrete evidence of your contributions and make a compelling case for your advancement. Whether it's a patent that drives product innovation, a publication that establishes thought leadership, or a trade secret that secures competitive advantage, the strategic use of IP can significantly enhance your chances for career growth.

WHERE SHOULD YOU PROMOTE YOUR WORK?

Everywhere—but mostly where your current manager, peers, and future colleagues will be able to find it.

For internal promotion, take advantage of Confluence sites, Teams channels, Discord, or any other platforms your organization uses to communicate. Beyond these, here are specific ideas to amplify your visibility:

1. **Slack Channels**
   - Identify relevant Slack channels where your peers and leaders are active. Examples include team-specific channels, leadership-focused spaces, or channels for innovation and learning.
   - Share updates or insights in these spaces. Use concise messaging paired with visuals like screenshots or diagrams. For instance: "Just wrapped up a new feature demo for [PROJECT NAME]. Results are promising! Here's a quick look at [HIGHLIGHTED IMPACT]. Feedback welcome!"

2. **Email Newsletters**
   - Collaborate with your team or department to add your work to internal newsletters. These may highlight team achievements, upcoming launches, or major milestones.
   - If your company lacks newsletters, create one for your group, summarizing key achievements, learnings, and relevant work updates. Make sure it's visually engaging with links to deeper content.

3. **Company Intranet or Blog Posts**
   - Publish posts that discuss innovative solutions, or share lessons learned from recent projects. Use the blog to highlight how your contributions solve organizational challenges or improve processes. Example: *"How We Reduced Downtime by 50 Percent Using [Your Innovation]"*

4. **Lunch-and-Learn Sessions or Webinars**
   - Organize informal sessions where you present your work to a cross-functional audience. This not only increases visibility but also builds connections across teams.
   - Promote these events through calendar invites and on platforms like Slack or Teams.

5. **Recognition Platforms**
   - Many organizations have innovation boards, idea-sharing portals, or recognition systems (e.g., Kudos Boards or Fond). Use these to spotlight your collaborators.
   - Nominate your projects or those of your team for internal awards or recognition programs.

6. **Virtual and In-Person Town Halls**
   - During town halls, volunteer to present key takeaways from recent projects. If your company uses tools like Figma, Miro, or Mural, prepare visually dynamic overviews that capture attention.

7. **Dedicated Teams or Project Channels**
   - If leading an initiative, create a dedicated communication channel or group for regular updates. Encourage feedback and celebrate milestones to foster engagement.

8. **Interactive Reports with Analytics Dashboards**
   - Build and share dashboards via tools like Tableau, Power BI, or internal analytics systems that visually demonstrate the impact of your work. Offer short presentations during team syncs or department reviews.

9. **Interactive Internal Events or Expos**
   - Participate in or host an internal project fair or expo where employees can showcase their work. Include hands-on demos or interactive presentations to engage your audience.

10. **Recognizing Team Efforts on Public Channels**
    - Regularly highlight your team's successes on collaborative platforms. Ensure your messaging includes a "we" focus to reflect shared ownership. This cultivates goodwill and positions you as a supportive leader.

By being strategic and consistent in how and where you promote your work, you make it easier for the right people to discover and appreciate your contributions. Visibility within an organization often correlates with influence, opportunities, and career progression.

External promotion takes a little more thought. Some new professionals have a hard time understanding what you can discuss publicly and what can't be discussed publicly. Anything that is generally addressed in the zeitgeist is something that you can learn and discuss yourself. Commentaries on public papers, books, articles, and even training videos are excellent as conversation pieces and public discussion points. This means that most copyrighted material can be discussed once published with proper attribution. Be sure to provide attribution and reference the original publications or knowledge source. It is public once published.

Open-Source contributions and Standards contributions are typically public by definition, so it is fair game to discuss them openly and often. Be sure to provide proper linkbacks and attribution.

Patents are less straightforward. Once a patent is filed, it is typically made public by being posted in full to the US patent database within 6–18 months. When the content of the patent is available for viewing by the general public, it is usually fair game to discuss in great detail. Until such time, you will want to avoid discussing implementation and any novel aspects, but you can talk about the market and areas of learning in a more generalized way.

Trade secrets should not ever be discussed in detail or posted to social platforms. You will need to figure out a way to discuss what you have learned and your expertise in this area without putting your reputation or organization at risk.

SOCIAL POSTING

Social media is a valuable place to share career moves or catch up with former colleagues. It's an exceptional way to amplify your IP achievements. If you're not using LinkedIn, Medium, or other distribution platforms to highlight your IP successes, you're missing out on opportunities to shape your professional narrative, build credibility, and expand your influence.

I'm not recommending you start putting up personal posts or filling others' feeds with your political opinions (or worse, incessant marketing from your current employer). You do not have to be one of the talking heads we now see when we are scrolling.

I am advocating for you to start demonstrating expertise and insight in your field. Social media is one place with a very low barrier to entry where you can establish yourself as a thought leader by sharing your journey, the challenges you've overcome, and the lessons you've learned. Discuss your IP, even talking about the process you use to create new ideas or learn from someone else. By posting wisely you position yourself as someone who's doing the work and shaping the future of your industry.

Social media gives you a platform to tell your story the way you want it said. Whether you're filing a new patent, publishing an article, or speaking at a conference, sharing these milestones allows you to control the narrative around your career. This isn't bragging; it's establishing yourself in your field. The more you share real achievements, the more you solidify your presence in the field, and the easier it becomes for others to associate your name with your areas of interest and expertise.

If you need a formula for sharing achievements without sounding boastful, consider the research conducted by Alison Fragale, an organizational psychologist and author of *Likeable Badass*, who studied how to create likability in the workplace. Her research shows that likability in a professional environment is a combination of assertiveness and warmth. She goes on to describe two effective methods for sharing accomplishments without coming off poorly.

The first method is to use humor. For example, if I'm discussing a recent publication, I might say something like:

> *"My latest research on AI ties the quality of the output to the quality of the input—much like my productivity is directly tied to the quality of my tea."*

Then, I would dive deeper into the results of the research, keeping the tone light while delivering the information.

The second method is to express gratitude and recognize the contributions of others. For instance, I could say:

"Few people have been more influential in my professional journey than Debra Slapak."

Then, I would describe our most recent collaboration or publication, highlighting how her guidance or support made it possible.

Both approaches—adding humor or showing gratitude—help convey achievements in a way that feels genuine and collaborative rather than self-promotional.

Social media, especially LinkedIn, is an incredible tool for expanding your professional network and connecting with others who share your interests. When you post about your IP achievements, whether it's a new patent or an exciting speaking opportunity, it can open doors you didn't even know existed. Engaging with your network through likes, comments, and shares builds visibility. This may create opportunities to build relationships with peers, potential mentors, and industry leaders.

I've lost count of how many times someone reached out to me after seeing a post. The posts and comments become prompts for coffee with former colleagues and friends. They often lead to conversations with people I wouldn't have otherwise met. LinkedIn has led to new jobs, speaking engagements, and even publication opportunities for me. It's a way to spark connections.

When you're looking to advance your career, whether by seeking a promotion or a new job, recruiters and hiring managers often check your online presence. Social media platforms serve as an unofficial resume, one where you have complete control. A well-maintained LinkedIn profile with regular updates on your IP activity gives potential employers or decision-makers a clear picture of your contributions. It can be beneficial during job transitions, as it sets you apart from other candidates by showcasing what you are thinking about, problems you have discovered, concrete accomplishments, like the number of patents you've filed or the articles you've published.

Social media has given me a platform to mentor and be mentored by more people than I ever could have one-on-one. Whether through sharing tips or highlighting the "IP trick" that helped me, social media has surrounded me with a community of innovators who lift each other up. And that's what it's all about: using your platform to create opportunities for others.

So, stop shrinking away. Social media amplifies your achievements, helping you build a personal brand, expand your network, and showcase your expertise. You don't like LinkedIn? Not a problem. There are thousands of other communities out there, at least a handful for every field. Some (like ADPList) are just for being a mentor. Join one that fits you and start posting content.

7

USING IP TO CHALLENGE, INFLUENCE, AND TRANSFORM INDUSTRY NORMS

IP can be used strategically to challenge and transform long-standing industry norms. In my work, I've learned how to leverage IP to shift mindsets and drive change within an industry. An example of this was using external publications to challenge the prevailing norms around AI-driven customer data analysis, pushing for a move from an "opt-out" to an "opt-in" model for customer data usage.

INFLUENCING EXTERNAL CHANGE

In the AI and technology sectors, the default approach to customer data usage has traditionally been "opt-out." In this system, technology companies collect and analyze customer data for AI-driven insights *unless* customers explicitly choose not to participate (although they are often unaware that this is an option). While this model is legal and widely accepted, it raises significant ethical concerns about transparency, customer consent, and the protection of personal data. Many customers are unaware of their data being used in these ways, and even when they are informed, the process to opt out is often cumbersome.

Despite these ethical concerns, there was little movement within the industry to change this model. Companies are incentivized to collect as much data as possible, and few question whether the "opt-out" standard is the best approach for customers or the industry at large. To many of us in this space this was a systemic issue needing to be addressed.

To challenge this industry standard, groups of technologists turned to IP. Rather than limiting our advocacy to internal conversations, many of us took the issue public by publishing externally facing ethics standards around AI data usage. We used external publications as a tool for change. These publications outlined the importance of transparency, customer consent, and ethical AI practices, and they argued that an "opt-in" model, where customers explicitly agree to the use of their data, should become the norm.

One such publication, featured in Cognitive World Magazine and titled "Mitigating the Risks of Intelligent Automation: Bias, Worker Displacement and more," emphasized that ethical AI practices are a fundamental part of the design process. We advocated for a shift to "opt-in" consent models, highlighting that customers deserve to know exactly how their data is being used and should have control over whether they participate in such analyses. The companies we worked for agreed to shift their models. This was a small but meaningful win, aided by external pressure. We were only a single snowflake in an avalanche. However this kind of public discourse to create change.

Recently, I became deeply concerned about a growing problem in the service provider industry: their inability to work seamlessly across vendors. I realized that as we move into an era defined by AI agents, this fragmentation will only intensify.

The very tool designed to simplify collaboration—natural language—could instead amplify confusion.

Here's why. Each vendor speaks a different dialect of the same language. One company might use the word agent to mean an executable running on a device, while another uses agent to describe a human technician. So if an AI agent receives the instruction to "delete the agent," what will it do? Delete the software? or fire the person?

That's when I knew we needed to act. I founded CAT-MIP.org, the Consortium for AI Terminology for Managed and IT Pros, to bring service providers and vendors together before this problem spirals. Our mission is simple but vital: create a shared language that allows AI systems to interoperate, communicate, and collaborate safely. Without common meaning, there can be no common progress.

In another case, Kathleen Moriarty actively taught and advocated for a security standard that offered greater security benefits for the broader good, even though it conflicted with an existing standard backed by a major company.

> If I pushed mine in the standards-based forums, this competing specification that was still owned by a company would have some pressure to be contributed into a standard process too, and that would benefit the industry. If I just silently went away, there would have been no forcing function for them to do better and to make it an open standard.
>
> —KATHLEEN MORIARTY

By publicly advocating for better standards and holding competitors accountable, Moriarty created a "forcing function" that compelled action, ultimately leading to more effective outcomes for the industry.

INFLUENCING INTERNAL CHANGE

External pressure can also help motivate internal change. Alvarium, a project created by Steve Todd that I had the pleasure of working on, is a powerful example of an outside-in approach. Todd's idea centered on validating the confidence of data. By collaborating with marketing teams, we developed a campaign idea around the product. This effort led to the marketing team funding hardware for a proof of concept.

> The outside-in approach is so important . . . We had this idea, and we needed to get customers interested. By working on open source and talking about it publicly, we could build momentum, get funding, and even ship a server to a customer site in South America to prove that it worked. That external validation pushed the project forward internally.
>
> —STEVE TODD

The impact of these external efforts directly influenced internal project funding. A similar dynamic played out with the AI initiatives I mentioned earlier in this chapter. When ethical standards became a public conversation, it became evident that continuing with an "opt-out" model would raise ethical concerns and harm the company's reputation. Customers began asking more questions about how their data was being used, prompting internal teams to rethink their approach.

This proactive stance kept the company ahead of regulatory requirements and positioned it as a leader in setting new industry standards. By using external IP to spotlight ethical concerns, we drove meaningful change and positioned the company as a leader in ethical AI practices and customer data protection.

This example illustrates how IP, especially through external publications, can challenge and transform industry norms. Publicly advocating for change and using IP to frame critical conversations creates external pressure. Strategic use of IP not only protects innovations, but also influences industry practices, challenges the status quo, and drives systemic change.

By taking these messages to external platforms, companies can force critical conversations out into the open. The steady drumbeat of external publications on ethics has drawn attention from government entities, industry leaders, and customers, creating pressure for businesses to reconsider their data usage practices. It is becoming increasingly difficult to justify the "opt-out" approach as public opinion and emerging laws continue to push for transparency and consent.

8

CHALLENGES YOU MAY ENCOUNTER

By now, hopefully you agree with me that creating and leveraging IP is a worthwhile endeavor—but there are challenges. You will encounter personal challenges, such as lack of time, experience, and support. You will also run into professional challenges like navigating resistance, funding shortages, bias, and patent committees.

Let's tackle the challenges we impose on ourselves first.

SELF-IMPOSED CHALLENGES

Time: "Where Do I Even Find the Time for This?"

Most of us are already carrying a full load. Between work, family, and a thousand daily distractions, finding the time to create IP can seem impossible. I have struggled with this for decades. The key here is intentionality. Carving out even an hour a week dedicated to IP development can add up; building IP doesn't have to be a massive, time-consuming endeavor. It can be as simple as writing one hundred words at a time. What matters is consistency and commitment. You don't need to wait for the "perfect moment" because that moment may never come.

For those facing time constraints, it can also be helpful to integrate IP creation into regular work tasks. For example, many innovations come from solving problems for customers or refining processes within a product team. Documenting these solutions and carving out time to formalize them as shareable ideas can lead to valuable IP without requiring after-hours work.

Fear of Failure: "Who Would Want to Read What I Create?"

This is a huge one, and I've been there. The fear of failure is the voice that says, "What if no one hears?" or worse, "What if my idea isn't brilliant?" It can keep you from even trying.

Here's the truth as I have come to understand it: Everyone starts somewhere. You don't need to be the top expert in your field to create something valuable. Everyone has a unique perspective, and sharing yours through IP adds value in ways you may not see immediately. You will fail. A *lot*. Expect it and learn from it. Failure isn't the enemy; not trying is.

Lack of Support: "I Don't Have Anyone Guiding Me"

The path to creating IP can feel lonely if you don't have mentors or peers who understand the value of what you're trying to do. The reality is that many people around you may not be thinking in terms of IP, and it's easy to feel isolated. Mentorship and collaboration are key here. Find communities of like-minded individuals, form mentor circles, surround yourself with people, and then share your goals. They can provide the support system you need to stay motivated and navigate the process. Don't be afraid to ask for advice or feedback. The best part of IP is that it's often a collaborative process; lean into that. This has certainly worked for me, as the mentors featured in this book can attest.

Workaholic Tendencies

It may seem as if you need to devote your waking hours to the relentless pursuit of IP to remain remotely relevant. However, this is untrue. In fact, working efficiently and creating space for rest, personal growth, and connections is far more important than chasing every IP opportunity. Overworking may lead to burnout, narrow thinking, and missed opportunities to see the broader picture that often leads to the most innovative ideas. I learned this the hard way. Early in my career, at one start-up, I was so focused on showing up to every meeting and driving a release across the finish line that I failed to leave time for reflection. Only later did I realize that the real opportunity was not the features we shipped but a larger concept that could have leapfrogged the market.

One of the most overlooked aspects of achieving success is the importance of pacing yourself. Success in IP is not measured by many hours you work, but about how effectively you use the hours you have.

> It wasn't about working around the clock—it was about working efficiently during the time I had.
>
> —STEVE TODD

Todd didn't allow the pursuit of patents to consume his entire life. He often carved out time in the mornings to work on his inventions, ensuring his ideas were clear and well-documented. However, he balanced this with personal priorities, demonstrating that strategic effort often outweighs sheer quantity of work.

Beyond efficiency, pacing yourself allows time to build meaningful connections. Intellectual property creation doesn't happen in isolation. Many groundbreaking ideas come from conversations with colleagues, interactions with mentors, and insights gained through collaboration, as I've emphasized throughout the book. For example, Todd attributes over 90 percent of his patents to collaborative work with others and emphasizes how partnerships often trigger the creative spark necessary for innovation. If you're constantly overworking, you miss opportunities to connect with others, learn from their perspectives, and build relationships that can amplify your impact.

Another essential element is maintaining focus: Not all ideas or projects are worth pursuing. Taking the time to evaluate which opportunities align with your goals and values is crucial. Pursuing too many projects spreads your energy thin and diminishes the quality of your contributions. Focusing on fewer, high-impact opportunities enhances your work while freeing up time for the truly important things in life: family, friends, personal development, and relaxation.

For example, I once became fascinated by how quantum computing might transform our ability to proactively detect security vulnerabilities on edge devices. The concept was thrilling on paper; it had enormous potential. But in practice, the timing was wrong. The technology was years from commercial viability, and our company wasn't in the quantum business. So I set the idea aside and redirected my focus to initiatives that aligned with our immediate goals. That decision didn't kill the idea; it preserved its potential for the future while allowing me to make meaningful progress in the present.

PROFESSIONAL CHALLENGES

The Complexity of the Patent Process

Filing for a patent requires a detailed understanding of both the invention and the legal requirements for patentability, as discussed in chapter 3. The language of patent applications can be confusing, and the formalities involved are daunting, especially for those new to the process.

To overcome these hurdles, I benefited from mentorship with experienced inventors who helped me understand the technical language, formatting, and legal aspects of submitting patent applications. They taught me how to describe the novelty and utility of my inventions in a way that met the rigorous standards of patent committees.

For United States-based inventors, the USPTO has many resources to help small businesses and independent inventors navigate the complex process of securing IP. One key resource is the Inventors Assistance Center (IAC), which provides guidance on IP matters, helping inventors understand the requirements for filing patents and trademarks. The IAC offers support on technical questions, form preparation, and navigating USPTO processes. Additionally, the USPTO Ombudsman Program, Patents Ombuds Office, provides a point of contact to help resolve issues during the patent application process. These programs ensure that inventors, regardless of their experience or resources, have the support to protect their innovations and bring them to market.

Bias in Patent Committees

If you are lucky enough to be employed at an organization with a patent committee, one of the most significant challenges for many inventors, particularly women and underrepresented groups, is overcoming bias in patent committees. Patent committees are typically comprised of senior engineers and architects who often come from similar backgrounds, both in terms of experience and demographics. As a result, patents submitted by individuals who don't fit the stereotypical mold of an inventor may not receive the fair consideration they deserve.

Overcoming bias in patent committees is a systemic issue that requires both individual and organizational changes. Bias often manifests as favoritism toward established inventors or skepticism toward submissions from minority or underrepresented groups. At one company, I heard reviewers openly claim that design held no real value, and I watched high-impact patents from user-experience professionals get rejected outright for that reason alone. In other cases, I saw submissions dismissed solely because the inventor's title included "product management." And of course, as I mentioned in chapter 1, I've experienced it personally when an engineer jeered at my patent submissions *in front of me* simply because they came from me. This is problematic because they can discourage talented individuals from even attempting to file patents, knowing they may face an uphill battle to get their ideas recognized.

One way to address this issue is by implementing standardized evaluation criteria that focus on the technical merits of the patent submission rather than who submitted it. Some IP management platforms, such as Anaqua, can be configured to support anonymized workflows that mask inventor names and other identifying details during the initial review process. This simple change can significantly reduce bias by forcing evaluators to focus on the strength of the idea itself. Unfortunately, in many organizations, patents are still evaluated subjectively, with committee members placing undue weight on personal perceptions of the inventor. By establishing objective metrics for evaluating patent submissions, organizations can reduce the impact of bias and create a more equitable environment for all inventors.

Additionally, fostering a culture of mentorship and collaboration can help mitigate bias. When senior inventors take the time to mentor others, particularly those from underrepresented groups, it sends a signal that everyone's ideas are valued and that success is achievable. One strategy is to build relationships with key decision-makers on the committee or in the organization. You can ask for reviews before submission and gain proactive buy-in. In my experience, building relationships with mentors who have already navigated the patent process can help overcome the barriers that bias creates.

Bias in these settings is often more about the evaluator than the quality of the patent itself.

Lack of Training and Support

Another challenge many inventors face is the lack of formal training in the IP process. While larger companies may have legal departments or IP teams that support inventors, or marketing and PR teams that support people in thought leadership opportunities, smaller organizations or those without a focus on innovation may not offer the same resources.

To overcome this, I've found it helpful to create spaces for informal learning and collaboration. At one of my previous workplaces, we initiated "Patent Fun Fridays," where employees could bring their ideas, and we worked together to refine them into formal patent submissions. These sessions provided a supportive environment for people who had never filed a patent before, giving them the tools and confidence to move forward.

Training programs that demystify the patent process are crucial for promoting IP creation across all levels of an organization. This approach ensures that everyone, regardless of their technical background or position, has an opportunity to contribute to the company's innovation pipeline.

Building Credibility in a Crowded Space

Almost anyone can publish content online, making the field of thought leadership increasingly crowded. As a result, it can be challenging to stand out and gain recognition, even when your contributions are valuable. To build a reputation as a thought leader, you must produce high-quality work and find ways to amplify your voice and connect with the right audience.

Establishing credibility is a long-term investment. It is a sustained effort over time to create a portfolio of work that demonstrates your expertise. For those new to the field or just beginning to publish, it can be challenging to break through the noise and get your work noticed by influential industry leaders or decision-makers.

To get people to read your publications, you must go beyond just hitting "publish" and hoping for the best. You must pair your publications with podcast appearances, conference talks, webinars, and guest articles. Think of it like building a web—the more places you can link back to your work, the more likely it is to get noticed. If you're speaking on a podcast, mention your latest paper. When you're on stage at a conference, highlight key insights from your publication and point people to it. Write guest articles or blogs and use them to reference your original work. The idea is to create multiple ways for people to discover and engage with your content. The more places that lead back to your publication, the more visibility and impact it will have. Work smarter, not harder, to ensure your work doesn't sit in a vacuum.

Consider my recent series exploring how artificial intelligence is reshaping managed service providers. It began as a simple blog post several years ago—a short reflection on why service providers should start paying attention to emerging AI adoption trends. That seed grew into a series of published articles, each iteration refining the message and reaching broader audiences through *PCR Magazine*, *Computer Reseller News* (often referred to as *CRN*), and *Comms Business*.

From there, the content evolved again. I shaped it into a full webinar, *Implementing AI in Your MSP*, a format that invited conversation and application. The ideas sparked interest and led to an invitation to appear on the *Beyond the Horizons* podcast. The same material was then repurposed for keynote presentations across multiple industry events.

By the time I had shared, tested, and refined the ideas through all these channels, the core concepts had matured into something larger. That's when I gathered and expanded them into two books: *AI for MSPs* and *How to Innovate with AI.*

This is how ideas grow into a portfolio: one thoughtful iteration at a time.

Overcoming Criticism and Risk of Exposure

Publishing content exposes you to scrutiny from peers, competitors, and the general public. It can be intimidating, particularly for those who are early in their careers. Thought leadership requires a willingness to take risks and accept that not everyone will agree with your ideas.

Negative feedback, especially in front of a public audience, can feel like a punch to the gut. It's disheartening, and for some, it can be enough to make you question whether publishing is worth the hassle. Learning how to manage criticism constructively isn't just a nice-to-have skill; it's essential to have in order to grow as a thought leader. Research shows that our natural instinct when faced with criticism is to either defend ourselves or retreat, both of which can hinder growth. Instead, we need to reframe how we see feedback.

Instead of seeing criticism as a reflection of your capabilities, view it as an opportunity for growth. Feedback, even when it stings, can provide valuable insights that improve your future work. Building resilience in the face of criticism is key.

One of the most effective strategies backed by research is "self-distancing." Studies show that when you step back and view the feedback objectively, as though you were giving advice to a friend rather than receiving it yourself, you can better evaluate its merit without feeling attacked. This helps you keep your confidence intact and focus on the actionable points.

Another tip? Find a trusted circle of colleagues or mentors to review the feedback with you. Peer review can improve the quality of work and the ability to handle negative criticism. These trusted voices can help you sift through the feedback to retain what's useful and discard what isn't. And a note to the people in the back: not all criticism is valid; you don't have to entertain it all.

Criticism is part of the journey, as I know well. You would not believe the people who have been outright hostile toward me for producing content and daring to create ideas, the senior leaders who have told me I should know my place, and the trolls who post on my LinkedIn feed whom I end up blocking. The real test of a thought leader is in how you handle criticism, learn from it, and keep moving forward to become stronger, smarter, and more resilient. In the words of the great Anton Ego: "The average piece of junk is probably more meaningful than our criticism designating it so."

Access to Platforms and Publishing Opportunities

Getting your work published in high-credibility outlets like industry journals, respected blogs, or major conferences can feel like trying to break into a fortress. It's tough. These platforms often have stringent requirements and limited spots for new voices. Just because it's hard doesn't mean it's impossible. There are ways to get your foot in the door, and it all starts with being strategic about your approach to networking and publishing.

First, let's talk about strategic networking because the saying "It's not what you know; it's who you know" holds a lot of truth in the publishing world. Networking doesn't have to feel forced or awkward. Start by engaging with people in your field through industry associations, LinkedIn groups, and online forums specific to your industry. Share thoughtful insights, ask questions, and comment on the work of others. Building an authentic connection first without immediately pitching your work helps create a foundation of trust and respect.

Once you've built rapport, you may ask your contacts to review your articles. Peer reviews are key. When you involve others in the reviewing process, it improves both the quality of your work and your chances of getting published. Well-networked authors are more likely to get their papers published, thanks to the validation of having their work reviewed and endorsed by recognized experts.

Mentorship is another crucial element. Don't just network horizontally; seek out mentors who have already navigated the publishing world. Reach out to people whose work you admire and ask them to review your articles or offer advice on where to submit them. Also, find people in your field who have less time in the industry. They bring different perspectives and are exceptional at identifying places where your research or writing lacks context. Don't be afraid to reach out. Often, people are willing to help when they see your ambition and the effort you're putting in.

Another strategy is collaborative publishing. If you're new to the game, team up with someone who already has a track record. Coauthoring a paper or blog post with them can provide you with credibility by association. It also opens the door to larger, more influential platforms as you leverage each other's networks.

Building a portfolio slowly is okay. Start by getting published in smaller, niche outlets, and even consider hosting your own website. Every article, blog post, or conference appearance is a stepping stone. Over time, these smaller pieces add up; they will build your credibility.

And let's not forget about leveraging social media. Platforms like LinkedIn, Medium, or guest blog spots for known sites are excellent options for getting your voice out there. Professionals are more likely to read an article if it's shared by someone in their network. By sharing your own articles and insights on social platforms, you'll increase the visibility of your work and start attracting attention from editors, peers, and potential collaborators.

The bottom line? Gaining access to high-credibility publishing platforms is challenging, but by strategically networking, seeking mentorship, collaborating, and building a portfolio over time, you can absolutely break through. I began with small, niche outlets like *Scientific Computing* and *The Pragmatic Marketer*. Those early articles helped me develop my voice and credibility. From there, I moved to larger industry platforms like *Business Expert Press* and *CRN*, expanding both my reach and my confidence. And now, this publication, one that represents years of experience, relationships, and refinement, is being published by Columbia University Press, my dream publisher. You will do well playing the long game, building relationships, and ensuring the right people know who you are and what you're capable of.

CONCLUSION

IP as a Strategic Career Catalyst

The pivotal thing I've learned throughout my journey is that success doesn't happen by accident. Especially when IP is concerned, simply having good ideas or working hard isn't enough. You must be intentional, strategic, and relentless about creating and protecting your IP. This process is long and sometimes, complex, yes; but IP is a tool that can catapult your career, empower your voice, and open doors that would otherwise remain locked.

For many people, IP feels elusive, something reserved for "inventors" or "experts." That's only partially true: IP is accessible to anyone willing to work, identify problems, and craft solutions. Whether you want to get promoted, build thought leadership, or gain recognition, IP offers a measurable, objective way to demonstrate your value and capabilities.

Criticism, failure, and rejection are inevitable parts of the process. You might submit a patent that gets rejected or publish an article that doesn't get much attention. That's okay. In fact, it's more than okay; it's part of the learning curve. Build resilience by accepting that not every idea will succeed. What matters is that you keep going. Each failure brings you closer to a win.

One of the most fulfilling aspects of IP creation is that it elevates others along the way. As I've experienced in my own career, mentoring others in their IP journey can have a ripple effect, creating a culture of innovation and collaboration. Create IP groups at work, offer to review someone's patent submission, or host a workshop on the process of filing patents. When you mentor others, you're paying it forward, reinforcing your own knowledge, and expanding your network.

Some of my collaborators have shared so much with me, and I hope to have helped them as much in return.

And don't forget to lean on others when you need help. Seek mentorship from those who've been down this path. Ask for feedback on your ideas, involve others in your patent-writing process, and build relationships with experienced inventors. Mentorship isn't just teaching. It enables learning and growing together.

The best IP comes from identifying a gap and filling it. Be curious, observant, and always think about how your skills can contribute to solving more significant problems. Those who anticipate industry changes position themselves as leaders in their field.

So, what are you waiting for? IP has the potential to change your career and your life. It's an objective measure of your contributions, a badge of expertise that no one can take away from you. It requires action, and you must step up and take control of your career in a way that no one else can.

Start with a plan, build a process, and stay committed. You have the power to create IP that pushes your career forward and transforms your industry. Whether you achieve these goals through patents, publications, or new innovations, your contributions matter. And by building your own IP portfolio, you'll be creating a legacy of innovation, leadership, and impact.

Don't wait for someone to give you permission. Go out and create your own opportunity. Build your own boat. Your IP journey starts now.

APPENDIX A

Patent Filing Example

UNITED STATES PATENT APPLICATION

of

NICOLE REINEKE

and

ALEXANDER REINEKE

for

SYSTEM AND METHODS OF ELECTROMAGNETIC AUGMENTATION OF SYNTHETIC OBJECT COMPOSITION

TECHNOLOGICAL FIELD OF THE DISCLOSURE

[0001] Embodiments disclosed herein generally relate to electromagnetic signatures and to synthesizing electromagnetic signatures. More particularly, at least some embodiments relate to systems, hardware, software, computer-readable media, and methods for synthesizing characteristics, including electromagnetic signatures, of objects including living objects.

BACKGROUND

[0002] Electromagnetic (EM) radiation permeates space and may come from a variety of sources. Example sources of EM radiation include, by way of example only, radio transmitters, light bulbs, and the human body. EM radiation may also exist at a variety of frequencies or types such as, by way of example, radio, microwave, infrared, visible, ultraviolet, and X-rays.

BRIEF DESCRIPTION OF THE DRAWINGS

[0003] In order to describe the manner in which at least some of the advantages and features of one or more embodiments may be obtained, a more particular description of embodiments will be rendered by reference to specific embodiments thereof which are illustrated in the appended drawings. Understanding that these drawings depict only typical embodiments and are not therefore to be considered to be limiting of the scope of this disclosure, embodiments will be described and explained with additional specificity and detail through the use of the accompanying drawings, in which:

Figure 1 discloses aspects of a synthetic object configured to emit EM radiation operating in an environment;

Figure 2 discloses aspects of a system for capturing, synthesizing, and replicating EM signatures;

Figure 3 discloses aspects of methods for capturing, synthesizing, and/or replicating EM signatures; and

Figure 4 discloses aspects of a computing device, a computing system, or a computing entity.

DETAILED DESCRIPTION OF SOME EXAMPLE EMBODIMENTS

[0004] Embodiments disclosed herein generally relate to augmenting synthetic objects with electromagnetic (EM) signatures (e.g., EM fields/waves/radiation). More particularly, at least some embodiments relate to systems, hardware, software, computer-readable media, and methods for synthesizing EM signatures in synthesized objects.

[0005] AI (Artificial Intelligence) or generative AI (GenAI) is often used in the context of computer-generated simulations and synthetic objects. This allows many characteristics of animate beings, such as, by way of example only, voice, voice tone, word choice, speaking patterns, sentiment, and/or visual appearance to be simulated. Thus, a synthetic representation of a person, animal, or plant simulates attributes of the person, animal, or plant. Embodiments of the invention relate to simulating the electromagnetic signatures emitted by animate or living beings. Embodiments of the invention are discussed in the context of simulation, but may also be applied to emulation.

[0006] EM signatures, by way of example only, refers to EM fields and/or EM radiation and are aspects of how living organisms interact with their environment. Embodiments of the invention relate to replicating/simulating the EM signatures of living organisms in synthetic objects. This enables synthetic object to better mimic or simulate the presence of living organisms and better create an immersive or realistic experience.

[0007] To achieve an improved sensory experience, simulating detectable stimuli, such as EM signatures, is beneficial. Embodiments of the invention may be implemented a variety of applications including, but not limited to, simulating human-plant interactions, creating more lifelike robotic pets or humanoid companions, improving emotional depth in remote communication, and the like. Embodiments of the invention thus relate, by way of example only, to replicating or simulating EM signatures in applications, synthesized objects, and/or environments.

[0008] As demonstrated in plant-based research studies, animate objects and beings detect, respond, and/or react to electromagnetic signatures. Embodiments of the invention relate to synthetic objects (e.g., AI driven or software driven objects, whether virtual or physical) that are able to simulate or generate EM signatures. Adding EM signatures to synthetic objects may deepen the realism of the synthetic objects, improve remote communications in personal and professional contexts, and the like. Embodiments of the invention further relate to synthetic objects that may be configured to emit EM signatures that are configured to an existing context or that can dynamically adapt to changing contexts. For example, a pet robot may be configured to emit EM signatures and dynamically adapt the EM signatures being emitted in a manner that depends on a perceived mood or emotion (e.g., a sentiment) of a user, on environmental factors, or the like.

[0009] More generally, embodiments of the invention integrate EM signatures with software and/or hardware-based synthesized objects to replicate characteristics of living beings or other objects including their EM signatures. EM signatures are an integral part of interactions between living organisms and their environment, which may include other living organisms (e.g., human-plant interactions). Embodiments of the invention capture, store, and replicate EM signatures synthetically in one example.

[0010] Generally, embodiments of the invention relate to an EM enginesynthesis engine (also referred to as an EM engine) that may have access to or receive a variety of different data and other inputs. The EM enginesynthesis engine may be configured to generate a synthesized object that may include aspects of multiple distinct objects, which may be represented by metadata.

[0011] One aspect of the data used by the EM enginesynthesis engine relates to EM signatures. Embodiments generate a database of EM signatures that may be collected from different sources and/or different contexts or scenarios. As previously stated, EM signatures refer, by way of example, to electromagnetic radiation/fields that may emanate from an object, an entity (e.g., a person or other animate object), or that may be present in an environment.

[0012] Embodiments of the invention may collect and store EM signatures from a variety of sources using a variety of collection systems. Example systems that may be used to capture EM signatures on a variety of objects may include, but are not limited to:

Magnetometers: Measures magnetic fields, often used in geomagnetic studies or for detecting low-frequency EM fields;

Electroencephalography (EEG) Machines: Records the electrical activity of the brain, indirectly measuring EM fields generated by neuronal activity;

Electrocardiography (ECG) Machines: Detects the electrical signals of the heart, producing data on its EM activity;

SQUID (Superconducting Quantum Interference Device): Extremely sensitive magnetometer used to measure subtle magnetic fields, including those emitted by biological systems;

Multimeters with EMF Detection: Measures electromagnetic field strength and voltage in electronic devices and environments;

EMF Meters (Gaussmeters): Specifically designed to measure the strength of electromagnetic fields in a given environment, commonly used for safety assessments;

MRI (Magnetic Resonance Imaging) Scanners: Uses strong magnetic fields and radio waves to capture detailed images of the body, often detecting EM field variations in tissues;

Electric Field Probes: Measures the strength and direction of electric fields in a specific area, often used in laboratory settings;

Thermal Imaging Cameras with EM Sensitivity: Some advanced models can detect infrared EM radiation, providing insights into heat-related EM signatures;

Electromagnetic Spectrum Analyzers: tools for analyzing a wide range of electromagnetic waves, from radio frequencies to light waves, often used in scientific and industrial research;

Inductor: A passive electronic device used to store electric energy as magnetic energy;

Electromagnets: An electronic device that uses electricity to create a magnetic field; and/or

Advanced haptic systems: Full-body suits or vibrotactile interfaces that attempt to mimic the sensation of being surrounded by physical energy.

[0013] Electromagnetic signatures collected by these systems are stored such that they can be reproduced physically using, by way of example only, electrodes, antennas, heat sources, infrared emitters, blackbody simulators, or the like. These sources are referred to herein as emitters.

[0014] In addition to collecting the electromagnetic signatures, the electromagnetic signatures may be associated with context. For example, when collecting an electromagnetic signature of a person, the person may be asked questions such as how they feel, whether they are healthy, or the like. Other context information such as environmental context (e.g., weather, time, location, indoor/outdoor) may be collected and associated with the electromagnetic signatures. This type of context allows the electromagnetic signatures to be searchable based on context and generated by a synthetic object accordingly. In another example, an electromagnetic signature may be generated in an effort to bring about a change in a user. For example, a synthetic object may be configured to emit an EM signature consistent with happiness in an attempt to cheer up a user perceived as sad.

[0015] Figure 1 discloses aspects of an EM simulation system including a synthetic object, configured to emit an EM signature, operating in an environment. Figure 1 illustrates an environment 100 and a synthetic object 102 deployed in or operating in the environment 100. The synthetic object 102 may be configured to emit EM radiation 104, which is an example of an EM signature. For example, the synthetic object 102 may include or be coupled to an emitter.

[0016] Generally, the synthetic object 102 may be virtual, physical, software generated, or the like. For example, the synthetic object 102 may be illustrated as an avatar on a computer display that may be coupled with an emitter such that the EM radiation 104 may be "emitted" by the synthetic object 102. The synthetic object 102 may be a hologram, a physical device, or the like. The synthetic object 102 may include multiple distinct physical and/or virtual components that may each emit the same or different EM signatures.

[0017] The characteristics (e.g., frequency, wavelength) of the EM radiation 104 emitted by the synthetic object 102 may depend on an application and/or what the synthetic object 102 represents or simulates. The characteristics of the EM radiation 104 may also depend on a temperature and/or shape of the synthetic object being simulated. For example, if the synthetic object 102 is configured to simulate a person, the EM radiation 104 is configured to mimic the EM radiation associated with a person, which may account for a person's average body temperature, surface area, and/or emissivity.

[0018] Generally, the EM radiation associated with a person is infrared or thermal radiation related to body heat. Thus, the EM radiation may be in a range of 3 to 20 micrometers. A person may also emit other types of radiation, including radio frequency emissions, but this may be very weak.

[0019] If simulating a person, the synthetic object 102 (or its associated emitter or emitters) may be configured to emit infrared radiation in a range of 3 to 20 micrometers. In one example, the synthetic object 102 may include or be associated with an emitter that includes heating elements that may be set to simulate human temperatures, thereby emitting EM radiation similar to the EM radiation radiated by a person. In one example, the synthetic object 102 may include or be associated with a black-body emitter configured to emit EM radiation that is dependent on temperature. Depending on application, the synthetic object 102 can be configured to emit a desired EM radiation. The synthetic object 102 may also adapt such that the EM signature changes for various reasons, such as changes in the environment, changes in a user, based on a schedule, or the like.

[0020] The synthetic object 102 may also be configured to have a shape similar to the entity being simulated. For example, if emulating a person, the object 102 may be a mannequin or have curved surfaces to somewhat resemble a human shape or portion thereof. In another example, embodiments of the invention are more focused on simulating the EM signature rather than the shape of a person. This may allow the synthetic object 102 to be more compact if physical in nature. Further, as previously stated, the synthetic object 102 may be displayed on a display or have another virtual representation.

[0021] In one example, multiple synthetic objects 102 may be deployed in an environment. Each of the synthetic objects may be configured to emit the same or different EM signatures.

[0022] The ability to emit an EM signature that may correspond to a human may be based on a collection of EM data collected from one or more persons and stored in a database.

[0023] For example, the EM signature generated by a person may be collected over time and correlated to the person's health, emotions, environmental conditions (e.g., weather, temperature, location), and the like. This allows EM signatures to be correlated to emotion or mood and other factors. This may allow a database of EM signatures to be constructed and stored in databases 116. As a result, the EM enginesynthesis engine 110 can set and /or dynamically adapt the EM radiation 104 emitted by the synthetic object 102 based on data collected and stored in the databases 116. The selection of an EM signature from the databases 116 may also depend on factors of the environment 100, users in the environment 100, or the like. For example, if the environment 100 is a greenhouse, turning on an irrigation system may be detected and cause the emission of the EM radiation 104 by the synthetic object 102.

[0024] In one example, a client 114 may interact with the synthetic object 102 directly or via the EM enginesynthesis engine 110. The client 114, for example, may input instructions or characteristics into the EM enginesynthesis engine 110 via a user interface. The input is used to draw data or information from the databases 116 to construct the synthetic object 102. Thus, in one example, the EM enginesynthesis engine 110 may receive inputs 112 that may influence how the synthetic object 102 is configured, speaks, looks, emits EM radiation, and the like.

[0025] For example, the inputs 112 may include sound levels, temperature, location, event information, user sentiment data, role data, capability data, or the like. This information may be used to select the EM radiation 104 emitted by the synthetic object 102. As the inputs 112 change, the EM radiation 104 may also change. The client 114, in some examples, can also select or direct specific EM radiation 104 configurations.

[0026] The synthetic object 102 may have a variety of different configurations. The synthetic object 102 may be configured to communicate (e.g., using networking hardware, a display) with the EM enginesynthesis engine 110 and/or the client 114. This may occur in a wired or wireless manner. This may occur when the synthetic object 102 is docked (e.g., for recharging a physical object). The synthetic object 102 may have a processor or controller configured to cause an emitter (e.g., heater, antenna, electrode) to emit a desired EM radiation 104. When implemented in a computer, the synthetic object 102 may be a module that communicates with he the EM enginesynthesis engine 110 for configuration data and may be able to control an emitter.

[0027] Figure 2 discloses additional aspects of an EM simulation system. The EM simulation system 200 includes an EM enginesynthesis engine 210 (engine 210) configured to receive inputs 202 and interact with consumers 230, such as devices 232, which may include synthetic objects. The EM enginesynthesis engine 210 may include processors, memory, and other suitable hardware and may be implemented in an edge-system, a cloud-system, an on-premise system, in a client-server system, in a distributed system, or the like or combinations thereof.

[0028] In this example, the devices 232 may represent or include objects or synthesized objects configured to emit EM signatures (EM radiation, waves, or fields). The EM signatures emitted by the devices 232 may be identified or provided by the EM enginesynthesis engine 210 using various databases and/or the inputs 202.

[0029] The inputs 100 include data or information that may be used to build some of the databases 116 used by the EM enginesynthesis engine 210. For example, the primary source data 204 may include input or information from a participant (e.g., an animate organism) and/or an environment. The primary source data 204 may include metadata such as date of birth, mood, sex, body temperature, voice recordings, words, or the like. Some of this source data 204 may be collected via a survey or the like.

[0030] The EM signatures 206 is an example of a secondary source and may include EM signatures. In one example, the primary source data 204 and the EM signature 206 are collected contemporaneously and may be correlated or related in the EM enginesynthesis engine 210. The EM signatures 206 may represent EM radiation collected using collection systems discussed previously.

[0031] The environment/object metadata 208 is another example of a secondary source and may include data such as sound levels, temperature, location, description, event information, inferred score (e.g., sentiment scores using artificial intelligence analysis), and the like. The metadata 208 can be correlated or associated with the EM signatures 206 and/or the primary source data 204 where appropriate.

[0032] As the inputs 202 are collected and stored, they represent or correspond to EM signatures in a variety of circumstances. Thus, the EM signature of a user may be associated with metadata reflecting the scenario such as an emotion of the user (happy with plant growth), location of the user (in a greenhouse), temperature (ambient greenhouse temperature), location (inside, geographical location), age of user, and the like.

[0033] This allows the EM enginesynthesis engine 210 to dynamically generate or instruct EM signatures based on a current context. For example, if a synthetic object is generated as a companion to a user and the user is feeling sad (e.g., based on a detected sentiment), the synthetic object can be configured to emit an EM signature consistent with a happy feeling. Thus, the synthetic object can be responsive to external stimuli.

[0034] Thus, the inputs 202 represent data that may be collected and stored in the EM enginesynthesis engine 210. The inputs 202 may also represent a current context that allows a synthetic object to be synthesized or generated by the EM enginesynthesis engine 210 taking into account a current context. Thus, a current context may be used to select data in the databases 226 used to generate or construct a synthesized object or to produce data that can be consumed by one of the consumers 230.

[0035] In this example, the EM enginesynthesis engine 210 may have access to a variety of databases 226 (an example of the databases 116). The engine 210 can process, store, and synthesize EM inputs into actionable outputs.

[0036] The databases 226 are described by way of example and not limitation and may include a data store (a non-transient computer readable medium).

[0037] The EM database 212, by way of example, may include or store electromagnetic data collected from secondary sources (e.g., magnetometers, SQUID devices). In one example, the EM database 212 may include entries structured as follows:

Source:	This identifies an origin of the data (e.g., device identifier and location);
Date/Time:	A timestamp of when the data was collected;
Values:	An array of raw EM field values; and
Primary Source Key:	Links data to associated primary source records for contextual association.

[0038] The object database 214 may store a record of objects or entities that generate EM signatures and their metadata. In one example, the object database 214 may include entries structured as follows:

Primary Source:	An identifier of the object (or entity) producing EM signatures;
Object Type:	Specifies a type of the object (e.g. biological, electronic, environmental);
EMF:	An array of EM data tied to the object;
Metadata:	Metadata describing attributes of the object.

[0039] The secondary database 216 may be configured to store secondary sources of data and their relationships to primary sources. In one example, the secondary database 216 may include entries structured as follows:

Secondary Source:	An identifier for the secondary data source (e.g., environmental sensor, sentiment AI);
Primary Source Key:	Links back to a relevant primary source;
Location:	Geographic or spatial location where the data was collected.

[0040] The synthetic object database 218 is configured to store synthesized representations of objects based on EM signatures and metadata inputs. In one example, the synthetic object database 218 may include entries structured as follows:

Synthetic (Boolean):	Indicates if the object is synthesized;
EM Key:	Links to EM signature data from the EM datastore 212;
Secondary Key:	Links to secondary metadata for context in the secondary database 216

[0041] The feedback database 220 is used to capture user or system feedback such that synthetic object generation can be refined. In one example, the feedback database 220 may include entries structured as follows:

Unique ID:	Identifier for the feedback entry;
Primary Source Key:	Links back to primary data sources;
Location:	A spatial context of the feedback.

[0042] The user database 222 may be configured to manage user information, permissions, and associated metadata. In one example, the user database 222 may include entries structured as follows:

User Name:	Unique User Identifier;
Permissions:	Defines access rights and roles;
Metadata:	User-related attributes.

[0043] The historian 224 is configured to archive data and relationships for analysis and traceability. In one example, the historian 224 may include entries structured as follows:

Unique ID:	An identifier for each historical record;
User Name Key:	Links to the user that generated or interacted with the data;
Object Key:	Links to the associated object or entity;
Array:	An array of historical instances or actions for analysis.

[0044] The consumers 230 are typically configured to consume data processed or generated by the EM enginesynthesis engine 210. The consumers 230 may include devices 232. The devices 232 represent external systems, software, and/or hardware that consume data from the EM enginesynthesis engine 210. Synthetic objects may be examples of the devices 232. For example, virtual reality headsets, augmented reality devices, smart devices capable of displaying or simulating EM environments, wearable technology that reproduces synthesized EM signatures for user interaction, stand-alone devices configured to reproduce EM signatures in an environment, and the like or combinations thereof.

[0045] The system 200 represents a framework or pipeline for collecting, processing, synthesizing, and/or deploying EM data in environments, including synthetic environments. Embodiments of the invention allow EM signatures to be integrated into practical applications.

[0046] In one example, a synthetic object may be defined as a set of metadata, attributes and outcomes.

[0047] For example, a synthetic object may be defined to represent a gardener. The gardener may be defined to have voice data from a first object, a visual representation from a different object, and an EM field of a yet another object. When the synthetic gardener is invoked, turned on, or otherwise accessed (e.g., via software) and generated, these attributes are pulled from the databases (e.g., databases 116 or 226) and used for behaviors, interactions, and responses.

[0048] The EM enginesynthesis engine 210 can generate and deploy a synthesized object having various characteristics and able to emit an EM signature (e.g., using an associated emitter).

[0049] Figure 3 discloses aspects of a method for generating a synthetic object. The method 300 includes activating an synthetic simulator 302. Activating, accessing, or turning on the synthetic simulator (e.g., an EM enginesynthesis engine 210) is an example of or may invoke an initialization operation that enables the synthetic simulator to begin processing inputs and managing a synthetic EM environment. The initialization ensures that all components (e.g., databases, sensors) are connected and operations. A synthetic system may be simple and compact (e.g., a smartphone) or other device capable of producing electrical impulses and running operations or more complex such as a set of devices including satellite links, external devices, and internal devise that work together to produce or achieve an objective. For example, may synthetic objects can be used to produce or simulate a crowd.

[0050] Once the system is initialized, user permissions are checked 304. This ensures that the system and user access data and synthesized objects for which permission is had. User authorization helps comply with privacy and ethical standards

[0051] Next, the object being synthesized is identified or defined 306. This may include receiving input from a user related to the object or entity for which a synthetic EM field will be generated. The input may include settings selected in a user interface. For example, the user may select a directive to increase crop production my simulating exposure to their worker (e.g., the synthesized object) twice a day at watering time.

[0052] More specifically, an object may be a collection of variables. An object may be a concept that can contain zero or more sets of associated primary and secondary metadata. Object may range, by way of example, from physical devices to plants to human participants or environmental features. When identifying the synthetic object, metadata may be retrieved to identify the object type and relevant attributes. For example, in case of a synthetic persons, the synthetic object may include metadata such as:

Voice recording (as collected directly through electronic or other methods or as rendered through generative AI or other replay device),
Video recording (as collected directly through electronic or other methods or as rendered through generative AI or other replay device),
Gender and age 10-year-old,
Location 10 Roadway Ave, Newark, New Jersey
Positive caretake John Smith
Torturer: crow
Electromagnetic field variables
    Action: Emotional State
    During exposure to specific music vs John Smith present vs crow present: electromagnetic field: time.

[0053] Metadata can be mixed and matched to create new objects that have not previously existed. For example: the voice of Oprah would be matched with the video of a tree to generate a talking tree using generative AI and pair the talking tree with the electromagnetic field of the Dalai Lama in an attempt to create a synthetic object that exemplifies one vision of a calming being.

[0054] More generally, synthetic objects are synthesized from objects stored in the databases. This allows the synthesized object to take on a variety of characteristics, which are changeable. A user, for example, can change the voice or the appearance. The user may also change the EM signatures. The metadata associated with the objects using to generate a synthesized object may provide data that allows the synthesized object to be built. EM data or metadata, for example, may specify characteristics of the EM signature (e.g., frequency, amplitude, temporal characteristics (repetition, modulation waveform, transients), and the like that allow a specific EM signature to be emitted. Similarly, other metadata may be used to define other characteristics, actions, functions, and the like of the synthesized object.

[0055] In addition, the synthesized objects can be quickly adapted. For example, changing the EM signature may simply require providing different EM metadata. Further, the databases may be searchable such that EM data associated with various emotions, environments, or other factors can be identified and used. This may allow a user so specify an EM signature for a small room with a certain ambient temperature with no light. Many different synthesized objects can be generated by mixing and matching.

[0056] The method 300 may also identify 308 a current directive. The determines the task or objective for the current synthetic object. More specifically, a directive may include specific instructions such as replicating a real-world electromagnetic signature, creating a synthetic signature composed of one or more signatures, or experimenting with novel EM field patterns. The directive can instruct the system to emit a single signature, replicate an existing EM pattern or respond to environmental stimuli.

[0057] In one instance, a synthetic object may be generated to simulate an interaction with a gardener. The data stored would have a range of EM signatures determined to be "positive interactions" that were recorded in the context of a gardener feeding their plants. The synthetic object "positive gardener" would always emit EMs recorded in feeding interactions with the plants.

[0058] In another example, an interaction between two humans which have varied signatures and varied results. In an example where the stimuli from the environment is labelled as positive such as a positive tone of voice (this is common in data labelling available with generative AI), the synthetic object will emit a recorded signature associated with positive metadata. When the stimuli is negative (such as a negative tone of voice, yelling, or a plot point in a horror movie that is scary), a secondary signal may be generated to change the EM field outputs to match the tone or metadata of a negative interaction, which data may have been previously recorded.

[0059] In the method 300, the EM field values to be emulated are returned 310. The EM field values allow an EM signature to be generated and emitted. This is performed to retrieve that data needed to simulate or emulate the EM field or radiation. In one example, the EM enginesynthesis engine may access the EM database to retrieve predefined or real-time EM field values that align with the directive. This may include raw EM values, patterns, or synthesized data for emission.

[0060] Next, the EM field is emitted 312. More specifically, outputs (EM fields) are generated into the environment or to a target. A simulator may emit the EM field based on calculated parameters. The emission may be directed at a physical space, device, or user.

[0061] Feedback may be gathered 314 or collected. The feedback may include data on the systems performance and/or user/

environmental reactions to the emitted EM field. The feedback may include user reactions, environmental changes, or device responses. This data is stored in the feedback database for analysis and system refinement. The feedback may enable iterative improvement of the simulation operation. In one example, the feedback may cause a loop that allows the directive to be modified or refined.

[0062] EXAMPLE

[0063] In one example, a user desires to generate a synthetic object that simulates a human in a work environment. The ideal coworker would do the work and would have the 'feeling' of camaraderie—which may include aspects of tone, visualization, and the EM field for a human that aligns with the experience.

[0064] In one example, the coworker may be designed by AI via code, via graphical user experiences, or the like. The user assigns an object name of Alison to the synthetic coworker. Alison is assigned the following metadata:

the skills of a prompt designer. This is achieved by using the secondary source input of Generative AI (aka an OpenAI prompt which reads "You will act as a prompt engineering expert").

An object type of "human" (this is stored as metadata and assigns the visualization to a human form if the synthetic object is visualized as an avatar)

A language type of "English" (this is stored as metadata and assigns the LLM to be an English-language model)

An EM type as "human" (this is stored as metadata, and the synthetic generator will pull from the list of available Human EM models upon instantiation of the object

EM behavior as "modeled based on the tone of the conversation" (this is stored as metadata and will influence the selection of the

EM model to ensure the existence of multiple emotions so the EM field can be responsive); and

EM opt-in for feedback of "include" (indicates a behavior that will randomly ask the human interacting with the synthetic persona how they believe the Alison object "feels").

[0065] In operation, an employee may request the assistance of a prompt engineer. The employee accesses the "request an AI coworker" user interface and selects a coworker type of Prompt Engineer Alison.

[0066] The EM enginesynthesis engine may synthesize Alison by collating:

The GenAI LLM of English;

The voice model of human female;

The visual model of human female;

The EM from a human female with EM type of variant/responsive;

If there is more than one EM model of human type, EM models with variant values and metadata associated with emotion are returned;

If there is more than one model, EM model with highest feedback accuracy is returned;

Feedback accuracy can be calculated using any form of mathematics, but one example is:

 If EM model has been deployed and feedback was included:

  When prompted, did the human feedback match the "GenAI" predicted tone/feeling.

  If yes +1

  If no −1

  If near match +0,

Order models by score, highest to lowest;

Select model with highest score.

[0067] Alternatively, EM models may be segmented by the score related to a specific emotion only. In one example, EM outputs across multiple models may be synthesized.

[0068] An EM model with highest score feedback for "happy" or "excited" would be used for interactions with "happy" or "excited" perceived values (e.g., based on "sentiment analysis"; see https://www.airops.com/nlp-guide/how-to-analyze-sentiment-of-groove-support-tickets-chats-with-generative-ai).

[0069] EM model with highest score feedback for "negative" sentiment would be used to emulate EM fields during negative interactions. These may both exist within a single interaction and would be usable in tandem.

[0070] The employee starts to work on the assignment. The employee requests assistance from "Alison""(via chat, text, voice or video conversation, or in-person conversation with a robot taking on the synthetic persona of Alison). If the first interaction is neutral, the hardware associated with Alison produces the EM field associated with neutral emotion.

[0071] If user gets an answer that is not aligned with their intent, the user enters or otherwise communicates (or sentiment is detected) that they are upset (e.g., angry). Alison interprets this sentiment as "unhappy," and the back-end system dictates that the correct EM response to "user angry" is "conciliatory/sympathetic." Alison then returns text asking "how can I improve" and emits an EM field value that matches the highest-score feedback for "conciliatory/sympathetic."

[0072] The user and Alison continue to interact to return the prompt. When the prompt is complete, and the user acknowledges that the interaction is successful (through words, visual inspection of the user's face, or tone or other feedback mechanism), Alison interprets that the user is "happy" and the appropriate response to the sentiment is to also emulate joy or happiness. Alison emits that EM field associated with "happy".

[0073] The user is prompted to supply feedback on their perspective of Alison's performance and projected feelings on the interaction.

[0074] This feedback is stored in the Historian and used in future score analysis.

[0075] This patent protects the system and method of collecting electromagnetic signals from secondary sources, associating the signals with stimuli and/or metadata (including keywords, environmental behaviors, or situational details), and associating both the signature and the stimuli with one or more objects in a data store. Then in real-time or near real-time or on demand, when a synthetic version of an object is recalled or created, an electromagnetic field can also be generated during the desired time (based on event, keyword, timed, or always-on), creating an effect at scale that invokes desired outcomes.

[0076] Embodiments of the invention may be used with virtual or augmented reality devices or headsets. An emission module may be coupled to these devices or integrated into these devices such that synthetic EM fields can be generated in a multisensory environment.

[0077] Sensors can detect changes in a user's mood, environmental conditions, and the like. These changes by may be used to generate an EM field to enhance or counteract the feedback.

[0078] Further multiple objects may be simultaneously simulated by retrieving and synthesizing EM fields for each object.

[0079] In another example, farmers and gardeners often develop strong bonds with their plants. By associating a synthetic version of a person with their unique EM signature, a replica could be placed in a nursery or field to influence plant growth positively. For instance, a farmer could replicate their presence across vast fields using AI-driven holograms emitting their specific EM signature, helping the health and well-being of the plants.

[0080] A gardener could use a synthetic replica of themselves, programmed with their unique EM field, to "stand in" for them in a greenhouse. The plants may respond to the synthetic presence as if the gardener were there, potentially promoting healthier growth to EM fields that may augment the experiences of plants, animals, or humans.

[0081] In another example, synthetic replicas of living beings may be generated, such as AI-powered humanoids or robotic pets. These replicas can mimic physical appearance, voice, and behaviors. Embodiments of the invention further enhance their realism by causing the replicas to emit EM fields. For example, EM data may be recorded in advance and used in replicas.

[0082] Embodiments of the invention may also enhance remote communications. In one example, EM signatures may be associated with synthetic projections, such as holograms or telepresence robots or as an extension to an online call. This allows for the sensation of being in the same room as a person to be perceived, thereby enhancing the emotional depth of remote communication.

[0083] Embodiments may enable commercial and personal applications. Celebrities could capture their EM signatures and offer them as a product, alongside perfumes or other merchandise, to create a unique sensory experience. Positive or calming EM signatures could be marketed as a means to influence the mood of a room or individual.

[0084] Synthetic objects could be designed to emit specific EM signatures for compatibility testing in fields like social matching or team dynamics. For instance, interactions between synthetic personas could predict compatibility in scenarios like matchmaking or group assembly.

[0085] In another example, spaces may be equipped with devices that generate dynamic EMF patterns in sync with synthetic stimuli. These might mimic crowdlike conditions or emotional resonance. Combining advanced sound design, haptics, and simulated EMF fields might approximate the feeling of presence.

[0086] Embodiments, such as the examples disclosed herein, may be beneficial in a variety of respects. For example, and as will be apparent from the present disclosure, one or more embodiments may provide one or more advantageous and unexpected effects, in any combination, some examples of which are set forth below. It should be noted that such effects are neither intended, nor should be construed, to limit the scope of the claims in any way. It should further be noted that nothing herein should be construed as constituting an essential or indispensable element of any embodiment. Rather, various aspects of the disclosed embodiments may be combined in a variety of ways to define yet further embodiments. For example, any element(s) of any embodiment may be combined with any element(s) of any other embodiment, to define still further embodiments. Such further embodiments are considered as being within the scope of this disclosure. As well, none of the embodiments embraced within the scope of this disclosure should be construed as resolving, or being limited to the resolution of, any particular problem(s). Nor should any such embodiments be construed to implement, or be limited to implementation of, any particular technical effect(s) or solution(s). Finally, it is not required that any embodiment implement any of the advantageous and unexpected effects disclosed herein.

[0087] The following is a discussion of aspects of example operating environments for various embodiments. This discussion is not intended to limit the scope of the claims or this disclosure, or the applicability of the embodiments, in any way.

[0088] In general, embodiments may be implemented in connection with systems, software, and components that individually and/or collectively implement, and/or cause the implementation of: synthetic object generation operations, EM signature emission operations, EM signature collection operations and the like, or combinations thereof. More generally, the scope of this disclosure embraces any operating environment in which the disclosed concepts may be useful.

[0089] New and/or modified data collected and/or generated in connection with some embodiments, may be stored in a data storage environment that may take the form of a public or private cloud storage environment, an on-premises storage environment, and hybrid storage environments that include public and private elements. Any of these example storage environments may be partly, or completely, virtualized. The storage environment may comprise, or consist of, a data center that is operable and that performs operations initiated by one or more clients or other elements of the operating environment.

[0090] Example cloud computing environments, which may or may not be public, include storage environments that may provide data protection functionality for one or more clients. Another example of a cloud computing environment is one in which processing, data processing, and other, services may be performed on behalf of one or more clients. More generally, however, the scope of this disclosure is not limited to employment of any particular type or implementation of cloud-computing environment.

[0091] In addition to the cloud environment, the operating environment may also include one or more clients capable of collecting, modifying, and creating data. As such, a particular client may employ, or otherwise be associated with, one or more instances of each of one or more applications that perform such operations with respect to data. Such clients may comprise physical machines, containers, or virtual machines (VMs).

[0092] Particularly, devices in the operating environment may take the form of software, physical machines, containers, or VMs, or any combination of these, though no particular device implementation or configuration is required for any embodiment. Similarly, data storage system components such as databases, storage servers, storage volumes (LUNs), storage disks, servers, and clients, for example, may likewise take the form of software, physical machines, containers, or virtual machines (VMs), though no particular component implementation is required for any embodiment. Where VMs are employed, a hypervisor or other virtual machine monitor (VMM) may be employed to create and control the VMs. The term VM embraces, but is not limited to, any virtualization, emulation, or other representation of one or more computing system elements, such as computing system hardware. A VM may be based on one or more computer architectures and provides the functionality of a physical computer.

[0093] As used herein, the term "data" is intended to be broad in scope. Example embodiments are applicable to any system capable of storing and handling various types of objects, in analog, digital, or other form.

[0094] It is noted that any operation(s) of any of the methods disclosed herein, may be performed in response to, as a result of, and/or, based upon, the performance of any preceding operation(s). Correspondingly, performance of one or more operations, for example, may be a predicate or trigger to subsequent performance of one or more additional operations. Thus, for example, the various operations that may make up a method may be linked together or otherwise associated with each other by way of relations such as the examples just noted. Finally, and while it is not required, the individual operations that make up the various example methods disclosed herein are, in some embodiments, performed in the specific sequence recited in those examples. In other embodiments, the individual operations that make up a disclosed method may be performed in a sequence other than the specific sequence recited.

[0095] Following are some further example embodiments. These are presented only by way of example and are not intended to limit the scope of this disclosure or the claims in any way.

[0096] Embodiment 1. A method comprising: generating a synthesized object, by a synthesis engine, based on input received via a user interface from a user, wherein the input values relate to the synthesized object, determining a directive for the synthesized object, determining an electromagnetic (EM) signature and providing EM data for generating the EM signature, and emitting the EM signature based on the EM data using an emitter associated with the synthesized object.

[0097] Embodiment 2. The method of embodiment 1, further comprising initializing the synthesis engine such that the synthesis engine is configured to interact with and manage an environment in which the synthesis object is deployed, wherein the synthesis engine comprises an emitter configured to emit the EM signature.

[0098] Embodiment 3. The method of embodiment 1 and/or 2, further comprising checking user permissions to ensure that the user has permissions to generate and use the synthesized object.

[0099] Embodiment 4. The method of embodiment 1, 2, and/or 3, wherein the input includes settings of variables selected by the user or by default, wherein the variables include one or more of: a voice, a gender, an age, a location, an EM action, an EM exposure, and an EM time or combinations thereof.

[00100] Embodiment 5. The method of embodiment 1, 2, 3, and/or 4, wherein the EM action is an emotional state, the EM

exposure specifies an external stimulus, and the EM time determines a time during which the EM signature is emitted.

[00101] Embodiment 6. The method of embodiment 1, 2, 3, 4, and/or 5, wherein the synthesis engine comprises databases including one or more of: an EM database configured to store EM data collected from secondary sources, an object database configured to store records of objects or entities generating EM signatures and their metadata, a secondary database storing sources of data and their relationships to the EM data, a synthetic object database configured to store synthesized representations of objects based on EM and metadata inputs, a feedback database configured to capture feedback for refining the generation of synthetic objects, a user database configured to store user information, their permissions, and metadata, and a historian configured to store data and relationships for analysis and traceability.

[00102] Embodiment 7. The method of embodiment 1, 2, 3, 4, 5, and/or 6, wherein the directive comprises a task or objective of the synthesized object.

[00103] Embodiment 8. The method of embodiment 1, 2, 3, 4, 5, 6, and/or 7, further comprising returning the EM data from an EM database, wherein the EM data is aligned with the directive or based on user or environmental factors.

[00104] Embodiment 9. The method of embodiment 1, 2, 3, 4, 5, 6, 7, and/or 8, wherein the user factors include sentiment data, wherein the EM data is changed based on the user factors.

[00105] Embodiment 10. The method of embodiment 1, 2, 3, 4, 5, 6, 7, 8, and/or 9, further comprising receiving feedback incorporated into subsequent generations of synthesized objects.

[00106] Embodiment 11 A system, comprising hardware and/or software, operable to perform any of the operations, methods, or processes, or any portion of any of these, disclosed herein.

[00107] Embodiment 12. A non-transitory storage medium having stored therein instructions that are executable by one or more hardware processors to perform operations comprising the operations of any one or more of embodiments 1–10.

[00108] The embodiments disclosed herein may include the use a computer including various computer hardware or software modules, as discussed in greater detail below. A computer may include a processor and computer storage media carrying instructions that, when executed by the processor and/or caused to be executed by the processor, perform any one or more of the methods disclosed herein, or any part(s) of any method disclosed.

[00109] As indicated above, embodiments within the scope of this disclosure also include computer storage media, which are physical media for carrying or having computer-executable instructions or data structures stored thereon. Such computer storage media may be any available physical media that may be accessed by a general purpose or special purpose computer.

[00110] By way of example, and not limitation, such computer storage media may comprise hardware storage such as solid state disk/device (SSD), RAM, ROM, EEPROM, CD-ROM, flash memory, phase-change memory ("PCM"), or other optical disk storage, magnetic disk storage or other magnetic storage devices, or any other hardware storage devices which may be used to store program code in the form of computer-executable instructions or data structures, which may be accessed and executed by a general-purpose or special-purpose computer system to implement the disclosed functionality. Combinations of the above should also be included within the scope of computer storage media. Such media are also examples of non-transitory storage media, and non-transitory storage media also embraces cloud-based storage systems and structures, although the scope of this

disclosure is not limited to these examples of non-transitory storage media.

[00111] Computer-executable instructions comprise, for example, instructions and data which, when executed, cause a general-purpose computer, special-purpose computer, or special-purpose processing device to perform a certain function or group of functions. As such, some embodiments may be downloadable to one or more systems or devices, for example, from a website, mesh topology, or other source. As well, the scope of this disclosure embraces any hardware system or device that comprises an instance of an application that comprises the disclosed executable instructions.

[00112] Although the subject matter has been described in language specific to structural features and/or methodological acts, it is to be understood that the subject matter defined in the appended claims is not necessarily limited to the specific features or acts described above. Rather, the specific features and acts disclosed herein are disclosed as example forms of implementing the claims.

[00113] As used herein, the term module, component, client, agent, service, engine, or the like may refer to software objects or routines that execute on the computing system. These may be implemented as objects or processes that execute on the computing system, for example, as separate threads. While the system and methods described herein may be implemented in software, implementations in hardware or a combination of software and hardware are also possible and contemplated. In the present disclosure, a "computing entity" may be any computing system as previously defined herein, or any module or combination of modules running on a computing system.

[00114] In at least some instances, a hardware processor is provided that is operable to carry out executable instructions for

performing a method or process, such as the methods and processes disclosed herein. The hardware processor may or may not comprise an element of other hardware, such as the computing devices and systems disclosed herein.

[00115] In terms of computing environments, embodiments may be performed in client-server environments, whether network or local environments, or in any other suitable environment. Suitable operating environments for at least some embodiments include cloud computing environments where one or more of a client, server, or other machine may reside and operate in a cloud environment.

[00116] With reference to figure 4, one or more of the entities or systems disclosed, or implied, by the Figures and/or elsewhere herein, may take the form of, or include, or be implemented on, or hosted by, a physical computing device, one example of which is denoted at 400 in figure 4. AS WELL, WHERE ANY OF THE AFOREMENTIONED ELEMENTS COMPRISE OR CONSIST OF A VIRTUAL MACHINE (VM), THAT VM MAY CONSTITUTE A VIRTUALIZATION OF ANY COMBINATION OF THE PHYSICAL COMPONENTS DISCLOSED IN FIGURE 4.

[00117] In the example of figure 4, THE PHYSICAL COMPUTING DEVICE 400 INCLUDES A MEMORY 402 WHICH MAY INCLUDE ONE, SOME, OR ALL, OF RANDOM ACCESS MEMORY (RAM), NON-VOLATILE MEMORY (NVM) 404 such as NVRAM for example, read-only memory (ROM), and persistent memory, one or more hardware processors 406, non-transitory storage media 408, UI DEVICE 410, and data storage 412. ONE OR MORE OF THE MEMORY COMPONENTS 402 of the physical computing device 400 may take the form of solid state device (SSD) storage. As well, one or more applications 414 may be provided that comprise instructions executable by one or more hardware processors 406 to perform any of the operations, or portions thereof, disclosed herein.

[00118] Such executable instructions may take various forms including, for example, instructions executable to perform any method or portion thereof disclosed herein, and/or executable by/at any of a storage site, whether on-premises at an enterprise, or a cloud computing site, client, datacenter, data protection site including a cloud storage site, or backup server, to perform any of the functions disclosed herein. As well, such instructions may be executable to perform any of the other operations and methods, and any portions thereof, disclosed herein.

[00119] The described embodiments are to be considered in all respects only as illustrative and not restrictive. All changes which come within the meaning and range of equivalency of the claims are to be embraced within their scope.

CLAIMS

What is claimed is:

1. A method comprising:
   generating a synthesized object, by a synthesis engine, based on input received via a user interface from a user, wherein the input values relate to the synthesized object;
   determining a directive for the synthesized object;
   determining an electromagnetic (EM) signature and providing EM data for generating the EM signature; and
   emitting the EM signature based on the EM data using an emitter associated with the synthesized object.
2. The method of claim 1, further comprising initializing the synthesis engine such that the synthesis engine is configured to interact with and manage an environment in which the synthesis object is deployed, wherein the synthesis engine comprises an emitter configured to emit the EM signature.

3. The method of claim 1, further comprising checking user permissions to ensure that the user has permissions to generate and use the synthesized object.
4. The method of claim 1, wherein the input includes settings of variables selected by the user or by default, wherein the variables include one or more of: a voice, a gender, an age, a location, an EM action, an EM exposure, and an EM time or combinations thereof.
5. The method of claim 4, wherein the EM action is an emotional state, the EM exposure specifies an external stimulus, and the EM time determines a time during which the EM signature is emitted.
6. The method of claim 1, wherein the synthesis engine comprises databases including one or more of:

   an EM database configured to store EM data collected from secondary sources,

   an object database configured to store records of objects or entities generating EM signatures and their metadata;

   a secondary database storing sources of data and their relationships to the EM data;

   a synthetic object database configured to store synthesized representations of objects based on EM and metadata inputs;

   a feedback database configured to capture feedback for refining the generation of synthetic objects;

   a user database configured to store user information, their permissions, and metadata; and

   a historian configured to store data and relationships for analysis and traceability.
7. The method of claim 1, wherein the directive comprises a task or objective of the synthesized object.
8. The method of claim 7, further comprising returning the EM data from an EM database, wherein the EM data is aligned with the directive or based on user or environmental factors.

9. The method of claim 8, wherein the user factors include sentiment data, wherein the EM data is changed based on the user factors.
10. The method of claim 1, further comprising receiving feedback incorporated into subsequent generations of synthesized objects.
11. A non-transitory storage medium having stored therein instructions that are executable by one or more hardware processors to perform operations comprising:
    a generating a synthesized object, by a synthesis engine, based on input received via a user interface from a user, wherein the input values relate to the synthesized object;
    determining a directive for the synthesized object;
    determining an electromagnetic (EM) signature and providing EM data for generating the EM signature; and
    emitting the EM signature based on the EM data using an emitter associated with the synthesized object.
12. The non-transitory storage medium of claim 11, further comprising initializing the synthesis engine such that the synthesis engine is configured to interact with and manage an environment in which the synthesis object is deployed, wherein the synthesis engine comprises an emitter configured to emit the EM signature.
13. The non-transitory storage medium of claim 11, further comprising checking user permissions to ensure that the user has permissions to generate and use the synthesized object.
14. The non-transitory storage medium of claim 11, wherein the input includes settings of variables selected by the user or by default, wherein the variables include one or more of: a voice, a gender, an age, a location, an EM action, an EM exposure, and an EM time or combinations thereof.
15. The non-transitory storage medium of claim 14, wherein the EM action is an emotional state, the EM exposure specifies an

external stimulus, and the EM time determines a time during which the EM signature is emitted.

16. The non-transitory storage medium of claim 11, wherein the synthesis engine comprises databases including one or more of:
    an EM database configured to store EM data collected from secondary sources,
    an object database configured to store records of objects or entities generating EM signatures and their metadata;
    a secondary database storing sources of data and their relationships to the EM data;
    a synthetic object database configured to store synthesized representations of objects based on EM and metadata inputs;
    a feedback database configured to capture feedback for refining the generation of synthetic objects;
    a user database configured to store user information, their permissions, and metadata; and
    a historian configured to store data and relationships for analysis and traceability.
17. The non-transitory storage medium of claim 11, wherein the directive comprises a task or objective of the synthesized object.
18. The non-transitory storage medium of claim 17, further comprising returning the EM data from an EM database, wherein the EM data is aligned with the directive or based on user or environmental factors.
19. The non-transitory storage medium of claim 18, wherein the user factors include sentiment data, wherein the EM data is changed based on the user factors.
20. The non-transitory storage medium of claim 11, further comprising receiving feedback incorporated into subsequent generations of synthesized objects.

ABSTRACT OF THE DISCLOSURE

Synthetic object generation with electromagnetic augmentation is disclosed. Objects, including living objects, may be replicated as synthesized objects. The synthesized objects are configured using metadata and are configured to emit electromagnetic signatures to deepen a realism of the synthesized object and enhance connections and relationships.

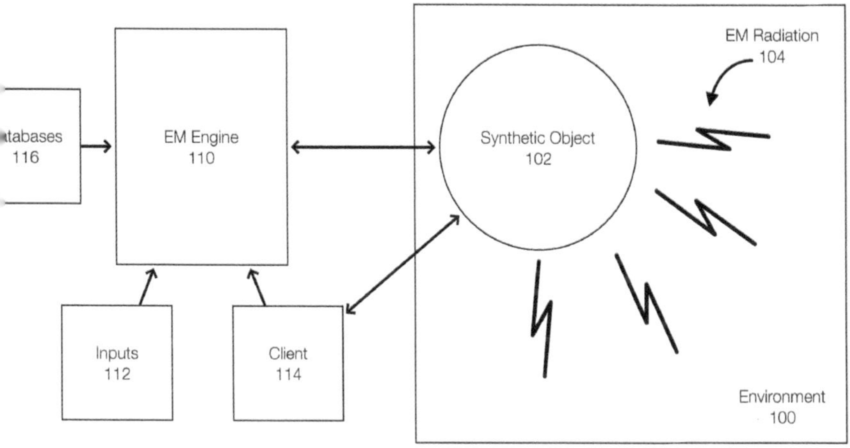

FIGURE A.1 Aspects of a synthetic object configured to emit EM radiation in its environment. (Illustration by Nicole Reineke.)

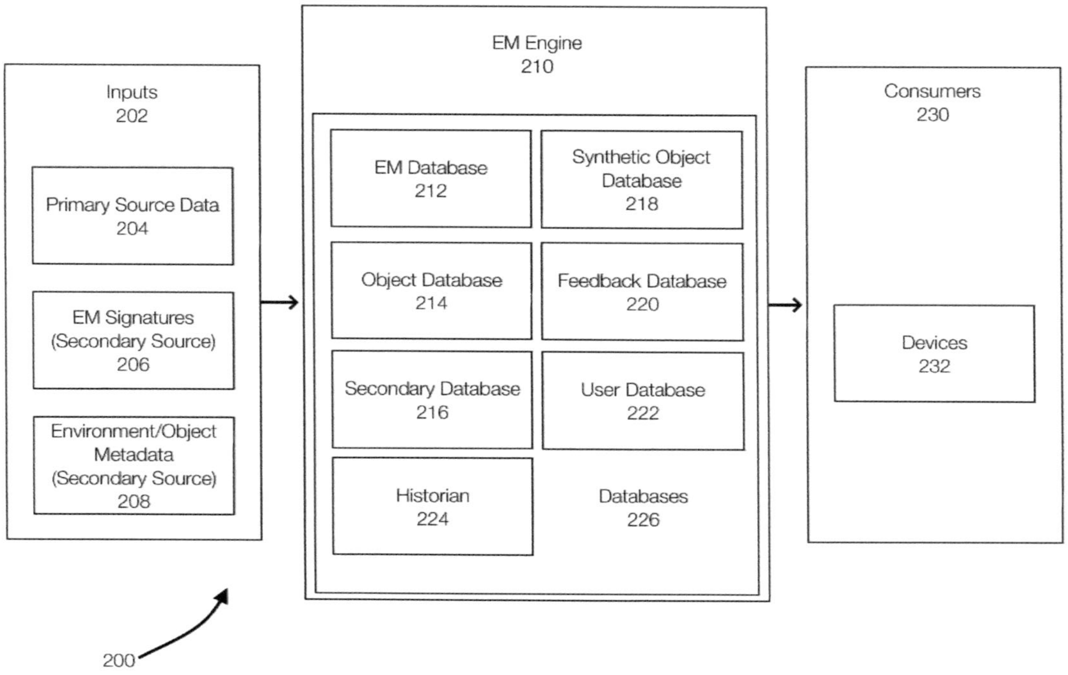

FIGURE A.2 Aspects of a system for capturing, synthesizing, and replicating EM signatures. (Illustration by Nicole Reineke.)

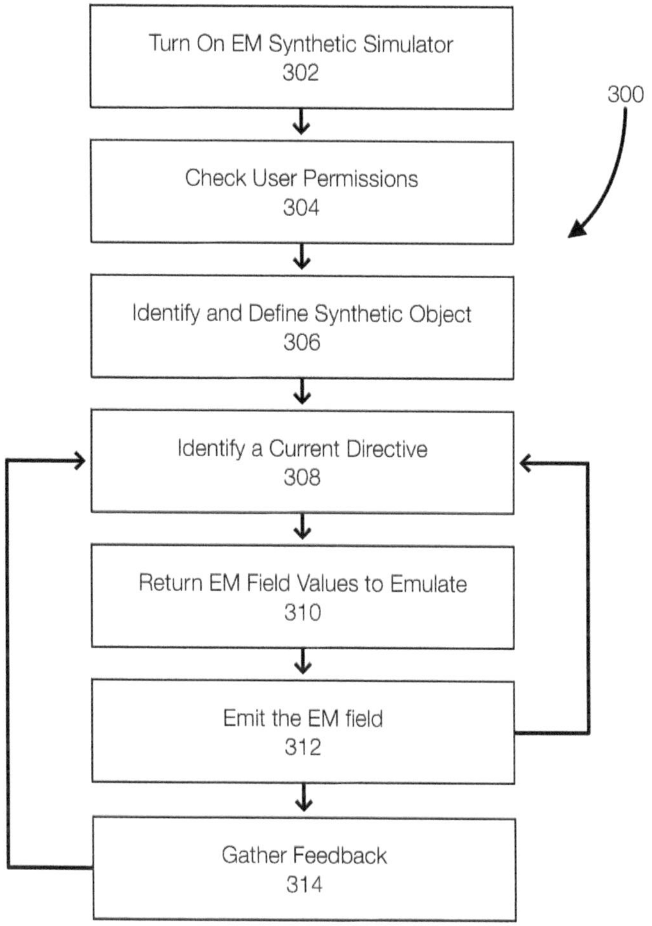

FIGURE A.3 Aspects of methods for capturing, synthesizing, and/or replicating EM signatures. (Illustration by Nicole Reineke.)

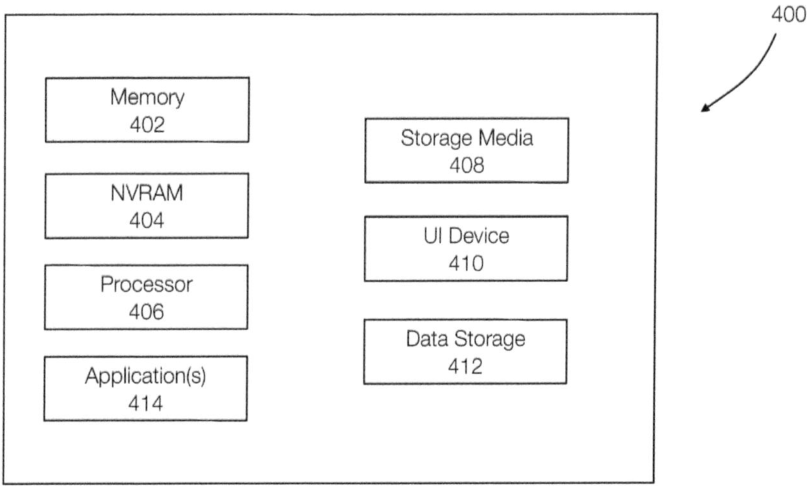

FIGURE A.4 Aspects of a computing device, a computing system, or a computing entity. (Illustration by Nicole Reineke.)

APPENDIX B

Draft Patent Disclosure Example

SYSTEM AND METHOD OF ELECTROMAGNETIC AUGMENTATION OF SYNTHETIC OBJECT COMPOSITION

Inventors
Nicole Reineke
USA

Alexander Reineke
USA

November 29, 2024 initial idea. Nicole Reineke Alexander Reineke
Dec 3, 2024 completion of workflows and dynamic synthesis Nicole Reineke and Alexander Reineke
Dec 6, 2024 extended workflows
Dec 9, 2024 added synthetic workflow detail
Dec 15, 2024 updated claims and workflow
Dec 23, 2024 review of claims and details
Dec 26, 2024 added squirrel example

ABSTRACT

Existing research supports the concept of plant responses to electromagnetic (EM) fields, suggesting that living organisms can perceive and interact with electromagnetic information. This foundation underpins the proposed system.

By bridging the gap between tangible replication of objects through the creation of composed (often AI-driven) objects (herein referred to as synthetic) and intangible electromagnetic presence, this innovation can deepen the realism of synthetic objects, enhance human connections, and unlock new possibilities in both personal and professional contexts.

OVERVIEW

This concept integrates electromagnetic (EM) signatures with software and hardware synthesized objects (herein referred to as synthetic) to replicate characteristics of living beings. EM signals are an integral part of interactions between living organisms and their environment, and these signatures can be captured, stored, and replicated in synthetic manners. As proven in plant-based research studies, animate objects and beings detect and respond to electromagnetic signatures. In the case of plants, they produce electromagnetic signals in response to environmental stimuli (https://theworld.org/stories/2014/01/06/can-your-plant-hear-your-can-it-think); these stimuli are detectable and can be replicated by non-animate systems. There is also research supporting that they also react to EM fields.

This patent protects the system and method of collecting electromagnetic signals from secondary sources, associating the signals with stimuli and/or metadata (including keywords, environmental behaviors, or situational details), and associating both the signature and the stimuli with one or more objects in a data store. Then in real-time or near-real-time or on demand, when a synthetic version of an object is recalled or created, an electromagnetic field can also be generated during the desired time (based on event, keyword, timed, or always-on) creating an effect at scale which invokes desired outcomes.

STATE OF THE ART

Currently, state-of-the-art research is focused on the detection of electromagnetic fields. Examples of machines that can capture EM data on different objects:

Magnetometers: Measures magnetic fields, often used in geomagnetic studies or for detecting low-frequency EM fields.

Electroencephalography (EEG) Machines: Records the electrical activity of the brain, indirectly measuring EM fields generated by neuronal activity.

Electrocardiography (ECG) Machines: Detects the electrical signals of the heart, producing data on its EM activity.

SQUID (Superconducting Quantum Interference Device): Extremely sensitive magnetometer used to measure subtle magnetic fields, including those emitted by biological systems.

Multimeters with EMF Detection: Measures electromagnetic field strength and voltage in electronic devices and environments.

EMF Meters (Gaussmeters): Specifically designed to measure the strength of electromagnetic fields in a given environment, commonly used for safety assessments.

MRI (Magnetic Resonance Imaging) Scanners: Uses strong magnetic fields and radio waves to capture detailed images of the body, often detecting EM field variations in tissues.

Electric Field Probes: Measures the strength and direction of electric fields in a specific area, often used in laboratory settings.

Thermal Imaging Cameras with EM Sensitivity: Some advanced models can detect infrared EM radiation, providing insights into heat-related EM signatures.

Electromagnetic Spectrum Analyzers: tools for analyzing a wide range of electromagnetic waves, from radio frequencies to light waves, often used in scientific and industrial research.

Inductor: A passive electronic device used to store electric energy as magnetic energy.

Electromagnets: An electronic device that uses electricity to create a magnetic field.

Advanced haptic systems: Full-body suits or vibrotactile interfaces that attempt to mimic the sensation of being surrounded by physical energy.

It's important to note that these devices and concepts exist; our invention does not claim the creation of these devices. It claims the association of electromagnetic information with metadata and stimuli in synthesized objects and the utilization of that electromagnetic information to direct the EM field emission in support of a synthesized object at scale with the intent to evoke a specific outcome.

PROBLEM BEING SOLVED

Current AI simulations and computer-generated synthetic objects can replicate many characteristics of animate beings, such as voice tone, word choice, speaking patterns, and visual appearance. These advancements enable synthetic representations to emulate the external attributes of a person, animal, or even a plant. However, these representations fall short in one critical area: they do not replicate the electromagnetic (EM) fields naturally emitted by living beings.

EM fields are an integral part of how living organisms interact with their environment. Without replicating this EM component, synthetic objects cannot fully mimic the presence of animate beings, limiting their ability to create a truly immersive or realistic experience.

To achieve a full sensory experience, it is essential to simulate all detectable stimuli, including EM fields. This is particularly relevant for applications such as enhancing human-plant interactions, creating more lifelike robotic pets or humanoid companions, and improving emotional depth in remote communication. The lack of EM field replication in synthetic representations is a gap this invention aims to fill.

USE CASES

1. **Plant Nursery Integration**

   Farmers and gardeners often develop strong bonds with their plants. By associating a synthetic version of a person with their unique EM signature, a replica could be placed in a nursery or field to influence plant growth positively. For instance, a farmer could replicate their presence across vast fields using AI-driven holograms emitting their specific EM signature, maintaining the plants' health and well-being.

   A gardener could use a synthetic replica of themselves, programmed with their unique EM field, to "stand in" for them in a greenhouse. The plants may respond to the synthetic presence as if the gardener were there, potentially promoting healthier growth to magnetic fields that may augment the experiences of plants, animals, or humans.

2. **Synthetic Replication of Once- or Currently-Living Beings**
   As technology advances, we are capable of creating synthetic replicas of living beings, such as AI-powered humanoids or robotic pets. These replicas can mimic physical appearance, voice, and behaviors. However, a key missing component is the association of electromagnetic signatures with these synthetic beings, which could enhance their realism and the emotional connections they facilitate. Imagine a robot that not only looks and sounds like a loved one but also emits an EM field similar to theirs.

3. **Enhanced Remote Communication**
   Remote interactions often lack the intangible feeling of presence. Associating EM signatures with synthetic projections, such as holograms or telepresence robots or as an extension to a Zoom call, we could recreate the sensation of being in the same room as a person, enhancing the emotional depth of remote communication.

4. **Commercial and Personal Applications**
   Celebrity Signatures: Celebrities could capture their EM signatures and offer them as a product, alongside perfumes or other merchandise, to create a unique sensory experience.
   Mood Influence: Positive or calming EM signatures could be marketed as a means to influence the mood of a room or individual.

5. **Electromagnetic Compatibility Testing**
   Synthetic objects could be designed to emit specific EM signatures for compatibility testing in fields like social matching

or team dynamics. For instance, interactions between synthetic personas could predict compatibility in scenarios like matchmaking or group assembly.

6. **Experience mimicry**
   Room-Scale EMF Emitters: Imagine spaces equipped with devices that generate dynamic EMF patterns in sync with synthetic stimuli. These might mimic crowd-like conditions or emotional resonance. Combining advanced sound design, haptics, and simulated EMF fields might approximate the feeling of presence.

INVENTION

The proposed invention includes a minimal viable system:

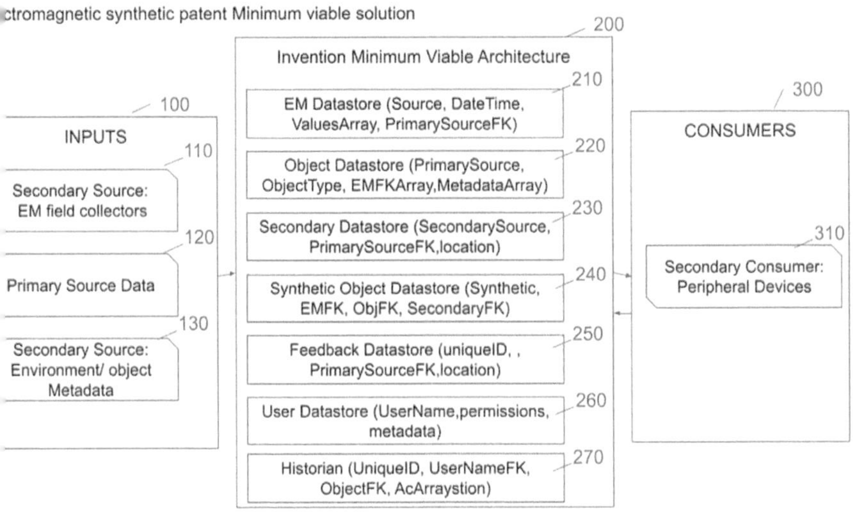

FIGURE B.1 Minimum architecture required for the invention. (Illustration by Nicole Reineke.)

1. **Inputs (figure 1, Label 100):** This section includes items and technologies that already exist that are used to inform the invention.
    a. Secondary Sources (label 110): EM signatures are captured from objects using well-known technologies.
    b. Primary Source Data (Label 120): Direct input from a participant and environment. For example, a person clicks a thumbs-up or -down button while in an environment where an electromagnetic signature of a human is being collected. Answers to survey results that ask them about their mood (the mood would be stored as metadata). Voice recordings, words, or video records (words would become metadata associated with an electromagnetic signature at a point in time). Data about the object such as male versus female, date of birth, or other.
    c. Secondary source metadata (label 120): For example, sound levels, temperature, physical location, descriptions, event information, inferred scores from secondary technologies (e.g., user sentiment scores from AI analysis).
2. **Invention Minimum Viable Architecture (Figure 1, Label 200)** This section details the net new architecture necessary to process, store, and synthesize electromagnetic (EM) data inputs into actionable outputs. It consists of multiple data stores, each serving a specific purpose within the system:
    a. EM Datastore (Label 210)
        i. Function: Stores electromagnetic data collected from secondary sources (e.g., magnetometers, SQUID devices)
        ii. Structure:
            1. Source: Identifies the origin of the data (e.g., device ID, location)
            2. DateTime: Timestamp of when the data was collected

3. ValuesArray: Array containing raw EM field values
4. PrimarySourceFK (Foreign Key): Links data to associated primary source records for contextual association

b. Object Datastore (Label 220)
   i. Function: Maintains a record of objects or entities generating EM signatures and their metadata.
   ii. Structure:
      1. PrimarySource: Identifier of the object producing EM signatures
      2. ObjectType: Specifies the type of object (e.g., biological, electronic, environmental)
      3. EMFArray: Array of electromagnetic data tied to the object
      4. MetadataArray: Associated metadata describing object attributes

c. Secondary Datastore (Label 230)
   i. Function: Stores secondary sources of data and their relationships to primary sources
   ii. Structure:
      1. SecondarySource: Identifier for the secondary data source (e.g., environmental sensors)
      2. PrimarySourceFK: Links back to the relevant primary source
      3. Location: Geographic or spatial location where the data was collected

d. Synthetic Object Datastore (Label 240)
   i. Function: Stores synthesized representations of objects based on EM and metadata inputs
   ii. Structure:
      1. Synthetic (Boolean): Indicates if the object is synthesized

2. EMFK: Links to EM field data from the EM datastore
3. ObjFK: Links to the corresponding object record in the Object Datastore
4. SecondaryFK: Links to secondary metadata for context

e. Feedback Datastore (Label 250)
   i. Function: Captures user or system feedback to refine synthetic object generation
   ii. Structure:
      1. UniqueID: Identifier for the feedback entry
      2. PrimarySourceFK: Links feedback to primary data sources
      3. Location: Feedback's spatial context

f. User Datastore (Label 260)
   i. Function: Manages user information, permissions, and associated metadata
   ii. Structure:
      1. UserName: Unique user identifier
      2. Permissions: Defines access rights and roles within the system
      3. Metadata: User-related attributes

g. Historian (Label 270)
   i. Function: Archives data and relationships for longitudinal analysis and traceability
   ii. Structure:
      1. UniqueID: Identifier for each historical record
      2. UserNameFK: Links to the user who generated or interacted with the data
      3. ObjectFK: Links to the associated object or entity
      4. AcArrayInstance: Array of historical instances or actions for analysis

3. **Consumers (Figure 1. Label 300):** This section outlines how the processed data is utilized by end-users or systems, emphasizing secondary consumers like peripheral devices.
   a. Secondary Consumer: Peripheral Devices (Label 310)
      i. Function: Represents external systems, software, or hardware that consume the processed data. Examples include: Virtual reality (VR) headsets or augmented reality (AR) devices. Smart devices capable of displaying or simulating EM environments. Wearable technology that reproduces synthesized EM fields for user interaction.

   This architecture provides a robust pipeline for collecting, processing, synthesizing, and deploying EM data in synthetic environments, bridging the gap between raw EM signatures and practical applications.

The synthetic object is defined as a set of metadata, attributes, and outcomes.

In one example you can imagine that I am defining a synthetic object to represent a Gardener. This Gardener may be defined by a software solution to have the voice data from a named object, a visual representation from a different named object, and the EM field of yet another named object.

When the synthetic object Gardener is invoked, or turned on, or otherwise accessed via software, these attributes are pulled from the data stores to form the behaviors and responses which the code will complete when accessed via API, code, or other electronic mechanism (such as voice command or physical stimuli like a haptic interface).

The interactions with the synthetic object Gardener will mimic the behavioral patterns of the sub-objects to form the cumulative response and new "synthetic behavior." Part of the synthetic behavior includes supplying the expected EM values in response to the stimuli.

SIMPLEST USE CASE

This diagram outlines the fundamental workflow for generating a synthetic object extension with Electromagnetic (EM) field simulation/generation. This workflow demonstrates how the system

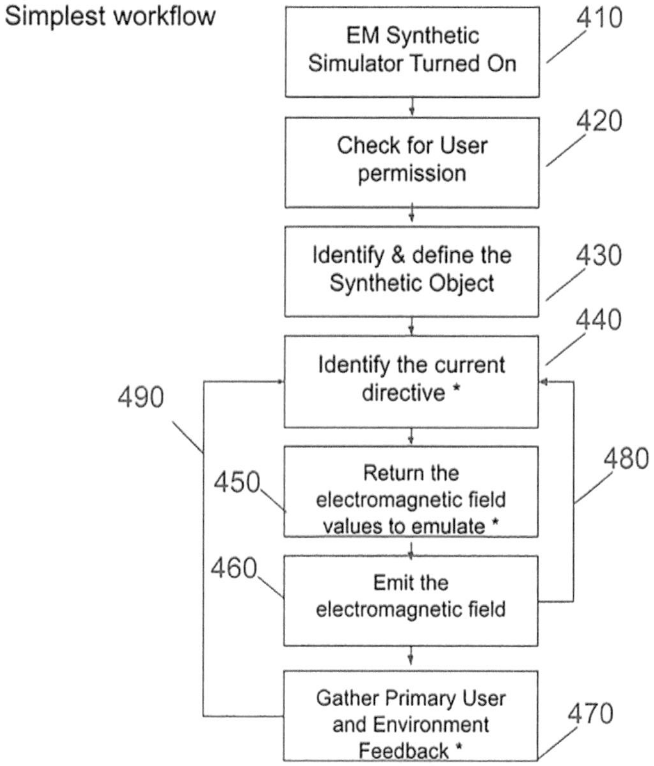

FIGURE B.2 Diagram titled "Simplest Workflow" including one end-to-end use case. (Illustration by Nicole Reineke.)

initiates, processes, and "composes" the synthetic object and then, using settings and sensors, determines the synthetic electromagnetic fields to emit using a secondary source, while incorporating feedback. Each step is labeled and explained as follows:

1. **EM Synthetic Simulator Turned On (Label 410)**
   a. Purpose: The process begins with the activation of the EM Synthetic system.
   b. Explanation: This step initializes the system, enabling it to begin processing inputs and managing the synthetic EM environment. It ensures that all systems and connected components (datastores, sensors, etc.) are operational. A system can be something as simple and compact as an existing iPhone or other device that is capable of producing electrical impulses and running software, or it can be as complex as a multi-device set of objects like a series of satellite links and external and internal devices which work in concert to product an objective. Many synthetic objects can be utilized to produce a "crowd."
2. **Check for User Permission (Label 420)**
   a. Purpose: Ensures that the user and system only access data- and field-synthesized objects, which they have permission to use.
   b. Explanation:
   c. User authorization is critical for compliance with privacy and ethical standards.
   d. The system verifies permissions, such as user preferences, access rights, and environmental data usage.
3. **Partially Novel: Identify the Object Being Synthesized (Label 430)**
   a. Purpose: Identifies values related to the object or entity for which the synthetic electromagnetic field will be generated.

This can be in response to settings selected by the user in an interface (such as: I would like to have an object that reminds me of my grandmother during Christmas) or could be hard-selected by a machine (such as: The machine directive is to increase crop production by mimicking exposure to their perceived caretaker John Smith twice a day at watering time).

b. Explanation:

i. Objects can be any collection of variables. An object is a "concept" and can contain zero or more sets of primary and secondary metadata associated with it. They could range from physical devices to plants to human participants or environmental features.

ii. Metadata from the Object Datastore (referenced in the architecture) is retrieved to identify the object type and relevant attributes.

In the case of a synthetic Person A, the Object may consist of metadata such as:

- Voice recording (as collected directly through electronic or other methods or as rendered through generative AI or other replay device)
- Video recording (as collected directly through electronic or other methods or as rendered through generative AI or other replay device)
- Gender and age: 10-year-old
- Location: 10 Roadway Ave., Newark, New Jersey
- Positive caretake John Smith
- Torturer: crow
- Electromagetic field variables
- Action: Emotional State
- During exposure to specific music (vs John Smith present vs crow present): electromagnetic field: time

– Metadata can be mixed and matched to create brand new objects that have not previously existed. For example: you could match the voice of Oprah with the video of a tree to generate a talking tree using generative AI and pair it with the electromagnetic field of the Dalai Lama in an attempt to create a synthetic object that exemplifies one vision of a calming being.

4. **Novel: Identify the Current Directive (Label 440)**
   a. Purpose: Determines the task or objective for the current synthetic object.
   b. Explanation: Directives may include specific instructions, such as replicating a real-world electromagnetic signature, creating a synthetic signature composed of one or more signatures, or experimenting with novel EM field patterns. It can instruct the system to emit a single signature, replicate an existing pattern, or respond to environmental stimuli.
   c. In one instance, you can imagine the synthetic object that wishes to simulate an interaction with a gardener. The data stored would have a range of EMs determined to be "positive interactions" that were recorded related to a gardener and feeding their plants. The synthetic object "positive gardener" would always emit EMs recorded in feeding interactions with the plant.
   d. In another case, you may have an interaction between two humans with varied signatures, thus leading to varied results. Where the stimuli from the environment is labelled as positive, such as a positive tone of voice (this is common in data labeling available with generative AI), it will emit the recorded signature with the positive metadata. When the stimuli is negative (such as a negative tone of voice, yelling, or a plot point in a horror movie that is scary), it would send a secondary signal to change the EM

field outputs to match the tone or metadata of a negative recorded interaction.

5. **Novel: Return the Electromagnetic Field Values to Emulate (Label 450)**
   a. Purpose: Retrieves the EM field data needed for simulation.
   b. Explanation: The system accesses the EM Datastore to fetch predefined or real-time EM field values that align with the directive.
   c. Includes raw EM values, patterns, or synthesized data for emission.
6. **Emit the Electromagnetic Field (Label 460)**
   a. Purpose: Outputs the generated or synthesized electromagnetic field into the environment or to a target.
   b. Explanation: The simulator emits the EM field based on calculated parameters. This is conducted by a secondary element and is not claimed as a novel invention of this pattern.
   c. Emission could be directed at a physical space, device, or user using specialized emitters or peripheral devices.
   d. We do not claim it is novel or that we invented the ability to emit EM fields; this exists.
7. **Novel: Gather Primary User and Environment Feedback (Label 470)**
   a. Purpose: Collects data on the system's performance and user/environmental reactions to the emitted EM field
   b. Explanation: Feedback may include user reactions, environmental changes, or device responses. This data is stored in the Feedback Datastore for analysis and system refinement.
   c. Enables iterative improvement of the simulation process
8. **Novel: Loop for Iterative Refinement (Label 490)**
   a. Purpose: Ensures continuous refinement by iterating based on feedback and directives

b. Explanation:
c. The system reevaluates the simulation parameters using feedback to improve accuracy and realism.
d. The system then returns to earlier steps (e.g., identifying directives or fetching EM field values) if adjustments are required.

9. **Novel: Final Output/Secondary Consumer Processing (Label 480)**
    a. Purpose: Sends processed EM field data and user feedback to secondary consumers or archives it for future use.
    b. Explanation:
    c. Data from this workflow can be utilized by peripheral devices or other systems for further applications, including VR/AR simulations, analytics, or scientific experiments.

MORE COMPLEX USE CASE

The user wants to generate a synthetic object that emulates a human in a work environment (as one may choose to do to with the rise of "AI coworkers"; see https://www.worklife.news/technology/ai-coworker/). The ideal coworker would do the work and would have the "feeling" of camaraderie—which requires aspects of tone, visualization, and the EM field for a human that aligns with the experience.

To achieve this, the AI coworker designer would generate a synthetic coworker. This can be done via code or a Graphical User Experience.

The human designs and then assigns the synthetic coworker object the name Alison.

Alison is assigned the following metadata:

- the skills of a prompt designer. This is achieved by using the secondary source input of Generative AI (aka an OpenAI prompt which reads "You will act as a prompt engineering expert").
- The Object type of "human" (this is stored as metadata and assigns the visualization to a human form if the synthetic object is visualized as an avatar)
- Language type as "English" (this is stored as metadata and assigns the LLM to be an English language model)
- **NOVEL:** EM type as "human" (this is stored as metadata, and the synthetic generator will pull from the list of available Human EM models upon instantiation of the object)
- **NOVEL:** EM behavior as "modeled based on the tone of the conversation" (this is stored as metadata and will influence the selection of the EM model to ensure the existence of multiple emotions so the EM field can be responsive)
- **NOVEL**: EM opt-in for feedback of "include" (indicates a behavior that will randomly ask the human interacting with the synthetic persona how they believe the Alison object "feels")

An employee requires the assistance of a prompt engineer. They access the "request an AI coworker" user interface.

The employee selects a coworker type of Prompt Engineer Alison.

The Invention synthesizes Alison by collating:

- The GenAI LLM of English
- The voice model of human female
- The visual model of human female
- **NOVEL:** The EM from a human female with EM type of variant/responsive
  - If there is more than one EM model of human type

- EM models with variant values and metadata associated with emotion are returned
- If there is more than one model
  - EM model with highest feedback accuracy is returned
    - Feedback accuracy can be calculated using any form of mathematics, but one example is:
      - If EM model has been deployed and feedback was included:
        - When prompted, did the human feedback match the "GenAI" predicted tone/feeling?
        - If yes +1
        - If no -1
        - If near match +0
      - Order models by score, highest to lowest
      - Select model with highest score
  - Alternatively, EM models may be segmented by the score related to a specific emotion only, in which case one may choose to synthesize EM outputs across multiple models.
    - EM model with highest score feedback for "happy" or "excited" would be used for interactions with "happy" or "excited" perceived values. This is a widely understood concept called "sentiment analysis"; see https://www.airops.com/nlp-guide/how-to-analyze-sentiment-of-groove-support-tickets-chats-with-generative-ai.
    - EM model with highest score feedback for "negative" sentiment would be used to emulate EM fields during negative interactions.
    - These may both exist within a single interaction and would be usable in tandem.

The employee starts to work on the assignment. They request assistance from "Alison" (via chat, text, voice or video conversation, or in-person conversation with a robot that takes on the synthetic persona of Alison). The first interaction is neutral, since the hardware associated with Alison produces the EM field associated with neutral emotion.

The user gets an answer that is not aligned with their intent. The user enters or otherwise communicates that they are angry. Alison interprets this sentiment as "unhappy" and the back-end system dictates that the correct EM response to "user angry" is "conciliatory/sympathetic." Alison returns text asking "how can I improve" and emits an EM field value that matches the highest score feedback for "conciliatory/sympathetic."

The user and Alison continue to interact to return the prompt. When the prompt is complete and the user acknowledges that the interaction is successful (through words, visual inspection of the user's face, tone, or other feedback mechanism), Alison interprets that the user is "happy" and the appropriate response to the sentiment is to also emulate joy or happiness. Alison emits that EM field associated with "happy."

The user is prompted to supply feedback on their perspective of Alisons' performance and projected feelings on the interaction.

This feedback is stored in the Historian and used in future score analysis.

CLAIMS

Patent Claims for "System and Method of Electromagnetic Augmentation of Synthetic Object Composition"

1. **Claim 1:**

   A system for capturing, storing, synthesizing at scale, and replicating electromagnetic (EM) signatures related to system objects, comprising:

A data collection module for capturing EM signatures from living or non-living objects using primary and secondary source mechanisms;

A database for storing captured EM signatures along with metadata such as stimuli, environmental behaviors, or situational details; and

Output for consumption of devices configured to emit EM signatures corresponding to the stored data, replicating an object's electromagnetic presence.

2. **Claim 2:**

   The method of associating EM signatures with metadata and stimuli, wherein:

   EM signatures are captured alongside keywords, emotional states, or environmental context;

   Metadata is stored in a database, creating a comprehensive profile of the object; and

   The EM signature is synthesized in response to specific triggers, such as a keyword, time-based event, or always-on configuration.

3. **Claim 3:**

   A system for replicating the electromagnetic presence of an animate or inanimate object in synthetic form, comprising:

   A mechanism for associating EM signatures with synthetic representations, including voice, behavior, and visual elements; and

4. **Claim 4:**

   A method of enhancing synthetic representations of living beings by integrating their unique electromagnetic signatures, enabling:

   Real-time replication of emotional or behavioral responses; and

   Enhanced realism in interactions between synthetic and living beings.

5. **Claim 5:**
   A method of the above where feedback is collected and used to train EM synthetic outputs to align with the intended metadata:

OTHER THINGS I WANT TO DO

1. Use this with VR and AR sets / make the emission module interface with peripheral devices, including virtual reality (VR) headsets, augmented reality (AR) systems, and wearable technology, to simulate synthetic electromagnetic fields in a multisensory environment.
2. Implement sensors to detect changes in user mood, environmental conditions, and object behaviors and drive back the EM field that is necessary to enhance or counteract the feedback.
3. Simultaneously simulate multiple objects by retrieving and synthesizing electromagnetic field data for each object from the data store (aka, imagine a concert where AI bots play off of each other, each simulating EM fields in response to the other).
4. Enhancement of remote bird feeder information or other monitoring systems—for example, you could imagine how much people already enjoy trail cameras—they get to see the animals as they pass by the location. Imagine being able to generate a synthetic replication of a squirrel or deer and actually have the "feeling" of the animals' EM field as they eat the bird food from the bird feeder. You could have this work with direct sensor transmission (what is sensed at the bird feeder is then emitted on the receiver), or you could have it synthesized based on the measured data from other squirrels as they took bird food and synthesized in the receiver.

APPENDIX C

Getting Started Workbook by Noell Ochieng

WHAT IS A PORTFOLIO?

A portfolio is a collection of external evidence that proves what you have accomplished. A strong portfolio consists of **intellectual property (IP)**, including patents, copyrights, open-source contributions, standards work, and other artifacts.

Your IP is what makes your expertise real, portable, and valuable no matter where you go.

Reflect and Respond

How does this list compare to what you thought IP was before?

____

____

Which types of IP sound most interesting to you? Why?

____

____

No matter where you begin, the key is to get started. Each step you take creates a legacy of knowledge and proof of your contributions, setting the stage for even more extraordinary achievements in the future.

—NICOLE REINEKE

HOW DO I BEGIN?

Patents: Find a problem, create a (possible) solution
Copyrights: Create content that serves a specific purpose
Trademarks: Create a unique name, logo, or design that sets a product apart
Standards: Enable interoperability, consistency, and scalability across industries
Open Source: Contribute to projects that excite you or align with your long-term goals.

Building a combination of IP can create an even stronger case for career advancement. When you present IP during a promotion discussion or job interview, you demonstrate that you are a technical innovator and recognized expert in your field. The strategic use of IP can elevate your career by providing undeniable proof of your skills and contributions.

—NICOLE REINEKE

You must be intentional in using IP to advance your career. IP is strategic, deliberate, and process-driven.

Try It Now

Consider an action or deliverable you created in the past; it does not need to be an example of IP. The purpose is to practice connecting your actions to business impact. Write it out as if it were part of an annual self-evaluation, a discussion with your manager, or an element of a job interview.

What I did:

____

____

____

____

Why it matters:

____

____

____

____

Business impact:

____

____

____

____

The following action verbs may help explain your achievements: accelerated, achieved, administered, advised, amplified, analyzed, assembled, built, catalyzed, championed, collaborated, conducted, coordinated, created, designed, developed, directed, elevated, enhanced, executed, facilitated, generated, impacted, implemented, improved, increased, initiated, innovated, instigated, launched, leveraged, managed, maximized, mentored, optimized, organized, overhauled, planned, produced, propelled, reduced, resolved, streamlined, supervised, transformed

PROMOTE YOUR WORK

IMPORTANT! Be aware of what you can and cannot disclose, especially to external audiences.

Platforms for Cultivating IP

INTERNAL

- Confluence, Teams channels, Viva, Slack, email newsletters, company intranet or blogs, lunch and learn, internal webinars

EXTERNAL

- Social posting—LinkedIn, Medium, Bluesky—as well as webinars and speaking engagements (in-person and virtual)

Recognition Platforms

- Interactive reports and dashboards, internal events or expos, recognizing team efforts on public channels, town halls

Challenges

PERSONAL

- Time
- Fear of failure
- Lack of support

PROFESSIONAL

- Complexity
- Bias
- Lack of training and support

REFLECT AND RESPOND

Which of the challenges listed do you think would be your biggest obstacle right now?

Why? What steps can you take to get past the challenge?

If someone close to you—a friend, child, your younger self—expressed this challenge, what would you advise them?

MAKE A PLAN

It takes as much energy to wish as it does to plan.

—ELEANOR ROOSEVELT

Take a moment and imagine yourself professionally five years from now. Write a short introduction of yourself briefly outlining your achievements and the impacts they have had on your organization, your field, and the people around you. Begin by listing examples of your future accomplishments; then use that to create an introduction.

Here's an example: *Mary Robinson has written articles for TechTarget and CRN and has spoken on the podcasts N-able, "Now that's IT," and Talk Python to Me. She is a lead software engineer specializing in AI security integrations and has spoken about the changing security landscape at the Empower industry conference. Mary balances her time between work, mentoring for Girls who Code, and family, including her dogs Fido and Spot.*

IP	Self-promotion/ Visibility	Other achievements

PROFESSIONAL INTRODUCTION

GOAL SETTING

Use your ideas from above as a launching pad. Select one element from your imagined introduction and create a SMART goal. Then break the goal into smaller, achievable objectives.

A SMART goal is a framework used to set clear and achievable objectives. The acronym SMART stands for:

- **Specific:** Clearly define what you want to accomplish.
- **Measurable:** Establish criteria to track progress and measure the outcome.
- **Achievable:** Ensure the goal is realistic and attainable.
- **Relevant:** Make sure the goal is aligned with your broader objectives and values.
- **Time-bound:** Set a deadline to create a sense of urgency and keep you focused.

Example:

GOAL

By <date>, I will submit a patent application for <idea>.

OBJECTIVES

By <date>, I will create a process sketch of <idea>.

By <date>, I will develop a Minimum Viable Product description for <idea>.

By <date>, I will download and review patent application documents to familiarize myself with the requirements.

By <date>, I will create a prototype for <idea>.

By <date>, I will consult with my company's legal team about our patent guidelines.

By <date>, I will submit the patent application for <idea> to our legal team/self-submit to the USPTO.

Try It Now

Goal

____

____

Objectives

____

____

____

____

____

____

____

____

Task Analysis

Breaking down a goal into objectives is a solid first step, but it does not end there. Next, consider what you need to reach those objectives. Ideas may include collaborating with others to bounce ideas around, working together to reach one goal, gaining access to tools or an environment, educating yourself about processes, or learning more details about specific elements of the industry landscape through journals, blogs, podcasts, YouTube videos, and publications.

Take a moment to consider and list what you need to reach a couple of the objectives.

Objective	Objective	Objective

How can you get what you need? Does it require building relationships, time, money, equipment? List proactive concrete actions you can take to get what you need to reach your goal.

____

____

____

Leverage Your Efforts

How can you get the most "bang for your buck" from your efforts? If you are writing a white paper, how can you use it to create multiple smaller works, like blogs, short articles, or social media posts? If you have created a trademarked graphic, is there a way to use elements of it for enhancing or creating other graphics, such as new color schemes or even a patentable technique used to create it? Explore some related ideas here. Write your main product in the center, and idea offshoots in the outside.

Scheduling

Conplete throwaway line. Creating time to work on your IP can easily get lost in the day to day of life. You need to deliberately schedule time for your future self to reap the benefits of your ideas and efforts today. You do not need to create a detailed schedule now, but there will need to be a tradeoff so that you can devote time to advancing your career. What is a low payoff activity you can exchange for this, a potentially high payoff effort?

Remember, we all need time to decompress and revive, so do not overreach. Use your time efficiently so you do not get burned out.

Pause and Reflect

How much time, and when, will you spend on reaching your professional goals to create IP and advance your career?

____

____

____

____

____

Congratulations! You are on the way to creating IP and furthering your career. You are an inspiration to others, and your work will improve our world.

> The future belongs to those who believe in the beauty of their dreams.
>
> —ELEANOR ROOSEVELT

Resources

Workbook created by Noell Ochieng based on resources from *Patently Successful*.

APPENDIX D

Mentor Biographies

WILL ALLEN

Will Allen is an innovator and inventor with over one hundred patents. His contributions, spanning groundbreaking technologies in physical printing to advancements in digital pathology, have left an indelible mark on major corporations like HP and Iron Mountain. For context, less than 1 percent of inventors throughout history have achieved this level of prolific success in IP creation.

Allen's impact extends far beyond his technical achievements; he embodies a rare combination of curiosity, collaboration, and mentorship that has shaped transformative products and the careers of countless individuals. Within the first year of knowing him, I witnessed him stand up an entire patent process within a global organization. Among his many initiatives, he single-handedly established a fast-track sustainability patent program that resulted in an international innovation contest, leading to several first-time inventors obtaining their first patents.

Allen credits his success to relentless curiosity and a drive for continuous improvement. He describes his approach to invention as "system-building," a skill he honed by identifying connections across diverse domains and applying them in innovative and impactful ways. His philosophy—that ideas are not finite, but are generated and enriched through collaboration—has been a guiding principle throughout his career. This ethos underscores his dedication to mentorship and community-building, as he consistently works to empower others to see the potential in their ideas and bring them to life.

With his work at Oregon State University, Allen inspires new generations of innovators to create and lead with curiosity, purpose, and a commitment to building something greater than themselves.

KATHLEEN MORIARTY

Kathleen Moriarty is a visionary in the fields of technology and security, with her career rooted in the meticulous and high-impact world of standards development. She is a titan in her domain, having invented the "Real Time Internet Work Defense" protocol—the first of its kind for internet tracebacks and incident response. As a former area director for the Internet Engineering Task Force (IETF) and a current board member for the Internet Society (ISOC), Moriarty is instrumental in establishing critical standards that continue to protect users worldwide.

Moriarty is the founder of SecurityBiaS (Built-in at Scale), a groundbreaking company at the forefront of security innovation that combines open source, standards, and intellectual property to redefine the future of technology and business. She has also served as the chief technology officer of the Center for Internet Security, where she further cemented her legacy as a leader in safeguarding digital systems through significant and unique thought leadership aimed at advancing security to better serve those with few resources. She is the author of *Transforming Information Security* and an adjunct faculty member at Georgetown University where she teaches and inspires future generations of security experts.

Her passion for standards is deeply tied to her belief in their capacity to serve the greater good. Moriarty's journey exemplifies how standards can act as a unique form of intellectual property that establishes professional credibility while driving systemic change. Her work underscores the profound impact of collaborative innovation and persistence, even in the face of resistance, to create a safer and more secure digital world.

Moriarty's career serves as a blueprint for anyone seeking to use their expertise to create meaningful, far-reaching change.

STEVE TODD

Steve Todd redefines what it means to be prolific. With nearly three hundred patents granted, his contributions are extraordinary. But Todd's creations don't stop there. He was a Technologies Fellow at Dell. He's authored books, published hundreds of blog posts and white papers, and spoken at industry events, all while shaping critical conversations around data innovation and strategy. His ideas have turned into tangible intellectual property, driving hundreds of millions of dollars in revenue through customer adoption.

What makes Todd stand out is both the scale of his contributions and his ability to connect and collaborate. Todd's openness in sharing his insights and creative process has amplified his influence far beyond his own company. One of his many notable achievements is gaining approval to open source the Alvarium project, a feat that highlights his exceptional ability to navigate corporate politics and push forward innovation in even the most traditional environments.

Todd's approach to IP creation is a masterclass in strategy. He seeks out complimentary skills to build on the power of collective knowledge. He keeps the long game in mind, noting that not every idea leads to immediate productization, but he values the ripple effects they create across industries and organizations. And by consistently delivering exceptional work, Todd built a foundation of trust that allowed him to tackle more ambitious and creative projects.

Todd's career is a testament to the power of intellectual property as a catalyst for transformation for entire teams. His humility, tireless work ethic, and commitment to collaboration have created a legacy of innovation and influence.

ANNE-MARIE McREYNOLDS

Anne-Marie McReynolds is a trailblazer in community building and technology leadership whose impact extends far beyond her own achievements. From her start as an investigative journalist, to a position of leadership at Dell where she ran a global patent committee, McReynolds has crafted a formidable technology career while identifying opportunities to advance equity and empower others. She is an innovator with forty patents filed and also a profound mentor, creating opportunities for underrepresented groups at a scale that is truly industry changing.

McReynolds's leadership as a mentor in the US Department of State's TechWomen program exemplifies her ability to connect IP with social impact. Under her guidance, women from over fifteen countries have solved culturally significant problems and pitched their innovative ideas to venture capitalists, including Amazon Web Services. Most recently, McReynolds mentored a team of five Pakistani women who created the winning pitch—an AI-driven platform designed to support the sale of handcrafted goods, a project that is aimed to have a profound impact on the ability of local women to support their families. In Pakistan, four out of five women are unemployed, and 81 percent of artisans are home-based women. Through her mentorship, these women have secured seed funding to build solutions that make a tangible difference in their communities.

One of the most significant impacts she has had on my career is the way McReynolds empowers her mentees to mentor others, creating a ripple effect that amplifies her influence. She has helped over a dozen individuals secure their first patents, ensuring they walk away with something tangible to bolster their careers. These inventors then go on to reach out to other team members and help them learn how to create career-changing IP. Her mentorship philosophy, "See One, Do One, Teach One," encapsulates her commitment to creating scalable impact.

McReynolds's career is a powerful reminder that innovation is not just about technology but about people. Whether she is guiding individuals toward their first inventions or shaping the future of inclusive technology, McReynolds's contributions are a masterclass in leadership, community building, and empowerment.

BILL PFEIFER

Bill Pfeifer is a master of connections and thought leadership, with a career defined by compelling stories that resonate across industries. As the host of a podcast on edge computing, Pfeifer brought together thought leaders from diverse domains, skillfully bridging technical insights with broader, relatable narratives. His storytelling doesn't just inform; it drives influence and action, creating real-world impact in ways few others achieve.

Pfeifer's talent lies in his ability to identify novel connections between seemingly unrelated fields. This ability to think beyond the obvious allows him to craft portraits that inspire action, such as his work connecting National Geographic's microplastics research to Dell's sustainability initiatives. Through this connection, Pfeifer didn't just tell a story—he catalyzed action, initiating a strategic partnership that reinforced Dell's environmental commitments.

A key aspect of Pfeifer's influence is his dedication to amplifying the work of others. He has a unique talent for turning individual contributions into leverageable thought leadership, as he did for me by elevating my work into a platform that expanded my visibility and influence. Pfeifer's knack for uncovering and championing promising ideas has also led to substantial investments in innovation projects, transforming technology stories into fully funded products.

Despite his far-reaching impact, Pfeifer is characteristically modest, rejecting the label of "thought leader" and focusing instead on enabling others to shine. His collaborative approach and his ability to weave technical expertise into accessible, powerful narratives make him a force for positive change across industries. Pfeifer's work exemplifies the power of intellectual property when paired with storytelling, showcasing how connecting ideas and amplifying voices can drive innovation and elevate entire fields. Whether by identifying hidden potential, championing sustainability, or amplifying diverse voices, Pfeifer offers invaluable lessons in influence, strategy, and connection.

ACKNOWLEDGMENTS

In memory of Johannes Reineke and Beatrice Ouellette.

To Debra Slapak, Will Allen, Anne-Marie McReynolds, Bill Pfeiffer, Kathleen Moriarty, and Steve Todd for your mentorship, wisdom, and generosity. You each taught me that innovation is as much about community as it is about curiosity.

To Roger Ouellette and Roseanne Ouellette for passing along the lifelong inability to stay in my lane or accept things simply as they are.

To my editor, Brian Smith, for sharpening my words and keeping me honest.

To my agent, Linda Konner, for believing in this work from the beginning.

To Carl T. Reed, my favorite patent lawyer. Truly, you won't find better.

To my colleagues Maggie Qian and Natasha Gaurav for years of joyful collaboration.

To my colleagues at N-able, Amanda Ray, Mike Adler, Laura Dubois, Darren Niller, for supporting my personal pursuits, and to Noell Ochieng, my extraordinary mentor-circle partner, co-host of the LinkedIn Live that helped refine these ideas, and creator of the workbook.

To my colleagues at Georgetown University, especially Carole Seargent for her guidance in publishing and Dr. Frédéric Lemieux for the opportunity to be part of the AI faculty.

To Anne-Marie Reyes Harvie, for her unwavering support of every writing and creative endeavor.

To Stephanie Brann for pretending my ideas are interesting over countless days out.

And to Gerhard, Alexander, and Lydia—always.

INDEX

GPSR Authorized Representative: Easy Access System Europe, Mustamäe tee 50, 10621 Tallinn, Estonia, gpsr.requests@easproject.com

www.ingramcontent.com/pod-product-compliance
Ingram Content Group UK Ltd.
Pitfield, Milton Keynes, MK11 3LW, UK
UKHW040448180926
475326UK00013B/10/J
9780231223829